M

A LIFETIME AGO:
BEFORE THE DEATH
OF CHILDHOOD

A Cautionary Memoir

Jeremy J. Joyell

A LIFETIME AGO
BEFORE THE DEATH OF CHILDHOOD

Copyright © 2008 by Jeremy J. Joyell

The views in this work are solely those of the author and do not necessarily reflect the views of the publisher, and the publisher hereby disclaims any responsibility for them.

ISBN-13: 978-1481254915

Printed in the United States of America

This book is dedicated to my wife Irene,
my sons Christopher and Michael, and
the class of 1956 from Bunker Hill Grammar School,
Waterbury, Connecticut.

1956 BUNKER HILL GRAMMAR SCHOOL GRADUATING CLASS COVER PHOTOGRAPH

Row 1: (left to right)   Raymond Ford, Robert Beaudoin, Aldonna Wedge, Philip (Graham) Beach, Carol Niemand, Sharon Collette, Kathleen Galvin, James Joyella, Patricia Wrynn, Robert Hallaway, Robert Birzell

Row 2:   Cynthia March, Sandra Pinski, Janet Tomasiello, John Cicchitto, Marcia Dalton, Sandra Strickland, Barbara Cozza, Russell Harlow, Christine Ingala, Elaine Waitkus, Elizabeth Rinaldi, David Dougall

Row 3:   Anthony Nardella, Romeyn Murphy, Michael Vignali, Joan Cook, Thomas Calo, Dorothy Fenn, Paul (Ricky) Lorton, Glenn MacBurney, Jeremy Joyell, James Lawlor

Row 4:   Henry Jeannin, William Grover, Carol Trombley, Porter Albert, Helena Platt, Barbara Violette, Diane Grover, Brian Somers, William Synnott, Thomas Clark

Row 5:   Sharon Gilchrist, Jo-Ann Murphy, Marion Murteza, Lorraine Caouette, Douglas Klish, Anita SantaLucia, Cecilia Mosgrove, Elaine Seebach

Row 6:   William Schofield, Timothy Phelan, Ronald Helps, David Beard, David Bartholomew, Mary Opalack, Peter Petrarca, John Migliorisi, Ralph Fabiano

Row 7:   Joyce Goudreau, Mary Mussa, Lorele Moran, Pamela Peper, Donna Muccino, Ann Fryer, Karin Peterson

Row 8:   Donald Soden, Nicholas Richards, Charles Harris, Howard (Randy) Ackerman, William Scavone, Richard Festa, James Sullivan, Edward Wells, Dennis Lackey

Acknowledgments

Many people helped bring this work to fruition. My wife Irene not only took on the Herculean task of word-processing and helped in editing, but had the even bigger job of putting up with me, my moods, my temper, my foot-dragging, and my continuing doubt about the whole project.

I also want to offer special thanks to my primary reader Professor Emeritus Milton Stern (University of Connecticut) as well as Professor Emeritus Paul H. Stacy (University of Hartford). Their evaluation, criticism, and praise were invaluable and encouraging.

I wish to thank all those readers of the manuscript who offered not only their reactions but also generously gave their time in plowing through the early drafts: Louis St.Amant, Prof. Al Avitabile, Phil Beach, David Beard, Anita Bologna, Patricia Brenner, John Buckey, Sandy and Joe Caggiano, Guy and John Colella, Jennifer Warner Cooper, Vera Dacey, Prof. Thomas Dulack, Patrick Finleon, Sharon Collette Flowers, George and Jim Greaney, Kathy Galvin Grimaldi, Al Joyell, Chris and Mike Joyell, Jim Joyella, Barbara Kane, Ilene Kaplan, Rose Kelly, Nancy Koekkoek, Dick Markowich, Harry Marsh, Maryellen Delaney McKeon, Tony Nardella, Janet Tomasiello O'Donnell, Vern Ouellette, Margaret and Susan Papa, Harriet Sauer, Bill Scavone, Bill Schofield, Rich Scortino, Dr. Ariane Sirop, Dennis Stanek Jr., Jim and Lori (Moran) Sullivan, and Bill Synott.

Finally I'd like to thank the class of 1956 at Bunker Hill Grammar School without whom this book would not have happened.

FOREWORD

Given the chance, if you could, would you choose to be a ten-year-old kid in *today's* world? That is the question I have asked scores of people over fifty years old in my travels all over our country. The virtually unanimous response was a resounding NO. Here I was offering them, with the help of my magic wand, an "opportunity" to shed forty, fifty, sixty years and become a kid again. Why they said no should serve as a wake-up call for any and all who are truly concerned about today's children. That is the reason I wrote this book.

Chapter 1

What if a much of a which of a wind gives truth to
summer's lie...

e. e. cummings

Nature had stretched summer's lie by at least one more day. September 21, 1996 offered a perfect morning, fitting and proper for those of us who were about to step back some forty years and visit with a past we still longed for.

Phil Beach and I trundled down Bunker Hill Avenue to meet with the rest of our eighth-grade classmates to re-create the graduation picture we had posed for June 19, 1956 on the steps of Bunker Hill Grammar School in Waterbury, Connecticut. There had been seventy-six of us then: the girls all crinolined in white, and the boys in charcoal gray suits, white bucks, white shirts and maroon ties (though the school color was green).

We turned into Farnham Avenue and nervously crossed the street to meet with all those "old" people who had instinctively gathered in front of the school at a spot that used to be shaded by a magnificent elm, now long gone, a victim of Dutch elm disease. Maybe an omen of another kind.

Thinking this was a mirror I might not want to look into, I held my breath, sucked in my stomach, and waded into the small crowd. Added wrinkles, extra pounds, less hair, gray streaks, but we still didn't need name tags. The smiles and eyes hadn't changed that much, but for me it was the voices, always the voices. Most were a little deeper, a little huskier, but I still could put a name and a face to a voice—blindfolded.

The tentative and giddy hellos immediately became handshakes and air kisses, which turned into long, hard hugs, real kisses, and

1

then tears of remembered joy and nervous laughter as we realized we were here, together again, safe and secure, if only for a day. The photographer herded us toward the steps beneath the portico as classmate Mary Opalack, referring to our graduation picture, tried to place us in the original positions to which we were assigned so many years ago. The good news was that we did it. The bad news was that there were originally seventy-six of us, and now there were only forty-five, and we needed a shoehorn to fit us between the white columns. Pictures taken, it was off to a barbeque that afternoon with hot dogs and "catch-up" and a dinner-dance that evening. At the request of the reunion committee, I had prepared remarks about the more humorous memories I had of those years, and our valedictorian, Kathy Galvin, talked about the circle of life and how reconnecting nourishes us and allows us to celebrate our lives with each other both then and for a few hours that evening.

Dinner eaten, glasses held high, school song sung ("O we are here/ Dear Bunker Hill/ To laud your glories to the sky . . ."), we gave the deejay a nod along with a caveat to play tunes released only between 1947 and 1956—kindergarten through eighth grade.

Between laughter and reminiscences the conversation naturally came around to kids, not specifically our own, but the entire next generation and how different they were from us. The usual gap we see from generation to generation had become more of an abyss. Long before NBC news anchor Tom Brokaw tagged our parents "the greatest generation," an assessment with which I have no quarrel, I began thinking that maybe those of us born between the thirties and the early sixties were the luckiest generation. "You kids don't know how lucky you are," was a constant mantra of my parents, relatives, and neighbors, usually accompanied by an admonishing finger waved in my face. It was true that many of the luckiest generation were either not yet born or too young to have felt the full force of the Depression or the savagery of the War, but by the mid to late seventies my thoughts about the great good fortune of my generation had nothing to do with the past. I began to see where things were going and sensed that a great part of our luck was not only in missing some of history's slings and arrows, but also being born early enough to avoid what was coming.

Slowly but surely the late sixties saw the beginning of a child-rearing philosophy that was alien to many of us. That kids change from generation to generation is a given. But over the last three or four decades youngsters have changed in fundamental ways in their behavior, thinking, and attitudes, changes that are both profound and disturbing. Any of us could come up with a litany of causes, some of which are our fault and some of which are simply beyond our control. But it seems we've become content in heaping responsibility for child behavior in places other than where it belongs—at the feet of the parents. All of my classmates confirmed what I had already found in my own unscientific poll of scores of people over forty: not one was willing to switch places with today's kids—a sad statement if you think about it. One classmate suggested, "They have no innocence." "They have been stripped of their childhood," volunteered another. This gathering was bringing to the fore more than fond memories for days long gone.

As my classmates vented their frustrations, I began to think about the outcry in the media for change—we needed new curriculum; teachers needed retraining; countless new programs had to be developed. The "experts," (most of whom had never been in a classroom or had left it as soon as they were able) all agreed. But most teachers who had witnessed the changes over the decades knew what was most needed—a different kid—one who had not been pummeled from all sides by a society that seemed to be losing sight of what kept kids focused, what was necessary to make them amenable to the learning process—the kind of kid whose numbers were rapidly diminishing—in short, the kid who could be taught.

Of course, implied in all this discourse was the haunting notion that in rearing our own children we seemed to have forgotten how we were raised. Ours was not a perfect society—none is, but ours worked pretty well, at least for kids. It seems we have now abandoned common sense only to embrace nonsense, and nowhere has it been more frustrating than for parents who are still trying to do their job the old-fashioned way, only to see their values eroded by a society that seems to act in a manner contradictory to all those beliefs.

The music had begun and I was thinking about getting out on the dance floor when someone suggested we shouldn't worry about the course our kids were following because "all things are relative." Interesting, I thought, how casually people invoke Einstein's thoughts and apply them to social behavior without realizing that he was talking about the world of physics. But in his famous equation, $E=mc2$, the letter "c" stands for the constant (the speed of light), and many of us seem to have forgotten that it was a life built around constants which gave us something to hold onto and still be kids. In our discourse I maintained that our security came from social and moral absolutes that placed limitations on our young egos. We were brought up in a world of fewer words and less rhetoric. There was a silent understanding of the rules. Sensing and knowing those parameters gave us freedom from the stress and confusion kids experience today. Simply and honestly put, I think that's why we learned so much more both in and out of school, and had a helluva lot more fun doing it.

As I was about to make one more brilliant pronouncement, my cousin, Jim Joyella, kicked me off my soapbox and cautioned us about getting too serious. He was right. This was a night for joy and laughter. I turned to find Diane Grover. Weeks earlier I had promised myself that she would be my first dance partner. I had taken her to a Boy Scout dance in sixth grade and had always felt guilty that I had somehow failed to walk her home.

I found her in the crowd, took her hand, and moved toward the dance floor. "It's about time," she said. "You never danced with me at the Boy Scout dance." Oh my God, a jerk times two. I think even Dante reserved a place in the lower depths for guys who do those kinds of things. I begged her forgiveness and pleaded that I had been a nervous wreck that evening of my very first date. Though I knew it was absolutely true, she probably wasn't buying it. She flashed a forgiving smile, but I could sense that all these years later a tiny bit of hurt still lingered.

Our conversation moved on to more mundane territory, but I couldn't shake the reactions we all had had a few minutes earlier about a generation gap too large to be bridged with traditional explanations. Maybe, I thought, the differences could best be explained by backpedaling about fifty years or so and taking a closer and, hopefully, somewhat more objective look at how those born during that three-decade stretch including the thirties through the fifties spent the first fourteen years of their lives—back to a time before the death of childhood. My feet fox-trotted forward, but my mind reeled backward. Diane and I reminisced. Billy Eckstine sang "I Apologize."

Chapter 2

. . . Be it ever so humble . . .

John Howard Payne

That ride to the reunion with Phil Beach actually began with another ride, a ride home from St. Mary's Hospital in Waterbury, Connecticut a few days after I was born on October 2, 1942, an event which my mother, Norma, never failed to remind me of whenever the opportunity presented itself, and sometimes when it didn't. I guess a baby just shy of eight pounds born to a five foot tall, ninety-eight pound woman will do that. I'm told the only positive observation my mother made about me that day was that I had a beautifully shaped head, which must be true because around age thirty-five nature began to expose more and more of it so that everyone could see that she was right. The ride home in my dad's 1940 black two-door Plymouth ended at 51 Wood Street in the north end of Waterbury, where the cobblestones beneath the pavement of the narrow streets still could be seen in the gutters. Originally named Mattatuck, it was an old New England industrial city of one hundred thousand tucked in the hills of the Naugatuck River Valley in west central Connecticut.

The war effort was in high gear, as were our factories. Waterbury, aptly dubbed "Brass Center of the World," was home to three giants of the brass and copper industry: Scoville, Anaconda-American Brass, and Chase Brass and Copper, my father's employer. The wartime employment of these three factories alone had swollen to twelve thousand as they had gone from manufacturing brass and copper products of every description to munitions plants overnight. "From lipstick cases to shell casings," as my dad's good friend, Kelly Longo, used to say.

Our house was my father's birthplace in 1909, right after his father had purchased it from a minister. A small three-family, it was virtually indistinguishable amidst a sea of multiple family urban houses, most of which were built during the turn of the century and now were beginning to look tired and faded. Though most were well-maintained, the grime from the nearby smokestacks clung to the paint of these less than attractive structures built more with an eye toward practicality than aesthetics, though much of what was soon to be slapped together to accommodate the imminent flight to the suburbs would look only slightly more appealing.

Though the house was sided with an asphalt shingle that was supposed to suggest yellow brick, it was nowhere near Dorothy and Toto's world. There was a tiny, no more than ten by twenty foot, swatch of grass in front guarded by a row of privet hedge. The driveway on the right was little more than a one-car wide patch of yellow cobblestone. There was no garage, primarily because there were no automobiles when these houses were built. Our car was kept four houses up the street behind the Perrone's house where there was a string of garages, each of which rented for three dollars a month.

With his father gone and his mother well along in years, my father was now responsible for the house. The first two somewhat larger floors were rented. Our third floor home was essentially a railroad flat. One would walk from the living room in the front, straight through my parents' bedroom to get to the kitchen in back, a fairly common arrangement in those days. My room was off the kitchen, just opposite the back door, which opened onto a long and narrow porch at the rear of the house. There was a tiny walk-in pantry behind the stove. All told there was little more than six hundred square feet of living space.

My paternal grandmother, Rose, lived in a small apartment attached to the left of the main house. She had it constructed at the end of World War I and opened a neighborhood grocery which she maintained until 1940, when it was converted to her retirement home (having lost her husband, Geremia, the grandfather for whom I was named, two years earlier).

The first floor was heated by a coal furnace in the basement. But the second and third floors had no such luxury. Their only heat was that provided by kerosene-burning stoves. Those beneath us had one in the kitchen and one in the living room. I suppose some of that heat rose to our place, but not much. We had a kitchen stove that also had a kerosene-fed heating unit, which was the sole source of direct heat for our entire apartment. I can still remember my father struggling with a five-gallon can of kerosene to place it correctly in the stove's receptacle. A mistake could mean instant inferno. At bedtime I would lie there and listen to the glug, glug, glug of the stove as it took huge gulps to feed the flame.

When you combine the single stove with the meager insulation provided by the cumbersome wooden storm windows with which my father would wrestle at risk of life and limb to hang outside our rattley double-hungs (and in the process introduce me to a new vocabulary), it's not hard to understand why he told me Jack Frost would "paint" the windows every winter evening. Sure enough, when I awakened each morning, the impish little guy, dressed, as I imagined him, like one of Santa's elves, had etched a tiny forest of fir trees along the bottoms of the windows in my room, just as my father had predicted. I wasn't really surprised. At that point my faith in my father's word was absolute.

No, it wasn't luxurious living; in fact, it would be generous to call it adequate, but as kids we are largely oblivious to such things. I had little interest in my surroundings other than the part they played in my discovering this strange and wonderful world that I was quickly becoming aware of. At any rate, this was to be my home for the first eight years of my life. All that counted was that we were a family and I was part of it.

Chapter 3

Only that day dawns to which we are awake.
Henry David Thoreau

I don't think we really begin to live, beyond the biological sense and our simplest Pavlovian responses, until we become conscious of the world around us and our place in it, though I'm not so sure we ever figure that out. Like most of us, I trace the "beginning" of my life back to my earliest memories—those bits and pieces of sights, sounds, tastes, and even smells; those early moments of our awakening that stay etched in our brain forever.

I "awakened" right around the time my brother Al joined our family in April of 1945. I don't remember his arrival, but I do remember the end of the war and my dad's presence. I didn't see much of my father until that time because he worked twelve hour shifts, six days a week, and sometimes was called in on Sundays as well. He was a mason by trade and was involved in the building and maintenance of furnaces critical to the production of brass and copper munitions tubing at Chase Brass and Copper. After we defeated Germany and it became apparent that victory over Japan was just a matter of time, the factory slowed a bit and he was home a little more often.

Late on a hot August morning he took me to the rear of the house onto our third floor porch that overlooked our backyard and a good part of the city. He sat me in his lap and told me that in a few minutes all the factory whistles would blow at the same time. The closest I had come to knowing anything about the war were my soldier doll, Buster, and the model of a B-17 Flying Fortress that hung from my bedroom ceiling. Though I didn't understand their significance, I do remember all the whistles blowing for what, to my young mind, seemed an interminable period. I remember my dad smiled and I even thought I saw a tear in his eye, but I had to be mistaken because I knew daddies didn't cry. That was August 15, 1945, V-J Day. At last the long horrible war was over.

The next day, like the rest of America, my dad was in a celebratory mood. My mother was occupied with my four-month-old brother, so Dad decided to take me to the Carroll Theater in the North Square to see *Pinocchio*. I shocked him thirty years later when I recounted events surrounding this brightest of my earliest memories, which I'm sure was very different from the kinds of visual experiences today's kids first have. Today's child is peppered with millions of images by age five, most rapid-fire and meaningless and not part of any cohesive context. Maybe the early television comedian and Renaissance man (actually quite a scholar), Steve Allen, was right when he noted that continuous doses of television would turn the brain to the consistency of white bread.

Those of us lucky enough to be born before television became a baby-sitter, parent, and source of all knowledge, were able to latch on to small but lasting images from books or an occasional movie (even from what our mind's eye conjured up from listening to the radio)—ones that could soothe or frighten, or could spark and feed our natural curiosity. These were few when compared to television's bombardments, but then we could savor the images, even, heaven forbid, think about them.

So there we sat in the balcony (that alone was a thrill) and up there on the huge screen were the first moving images I had ever seen. In a matter of minutes old Gepetto, Jiminy Cricket, Figaro, Cleo, and Pinocchio made me a lifelong film buff. To a kid born into a world without television, this was indeed a watershed moment, and though I didn't completely understand what was going on, in part because I was so overwhelmed by the medium itself, I perfectly remember three scenes in the picture, and one more which was to follow at home the next day.

I was horrified when Monstro the Whale swallowed Pinocchio, thrilled when Gepetto's wooden creation became the living son he had longed for, and was particularly terror-stricken when Pinocchio's nose grew long when he lied, a reaction which my ninety-four year old father remembered well to his last day. Above all, I can still clearly recall one moment the day after the film. I even remember where I was standing in our tiny kitchen when it happened. That morning my mother had asked me something of no real importance, but I "bent" the truth in my reply. My father, with serious visage and furrowed brow, still a long way from understanding his first child, reminded me that, if I fibbed, my nose would grow long. He was, of course, just kidding, but I began to bawl uncontrollably. It was at that moment, he later pointed out, that he first learned how seriously I took everything. I still live with that tendency, one that has sometimes been more curse than blessing. He immediately swept me up into his arms and apologized profusely, but still I sensed there was a lesson in there somewhere.

Decades later I realized it's difficult for young parents to see how deeply such seemingly minor events can touch a child's spirit and soul, heighten his sense of wonderment, or set fire to a young imagination and evolving intellect. I don't mean, however, that a young mom or dad should fret over every parental faux pas; in fact, today's preoccupation with hypersensitivity only exacerbates the situation.

My little episode actually informed two aspects of my life: One said something about morality and the consequences of lying; the other taught me something about developing a good sense of humor, specifically, how to take a kidding.

This was a preliminary to my earliest pre-school education. The serious side of me got a little lesson about sometimes being less serious, but the romantic in me still gets teary-eyed when I hear Jiminy Cricket sing "When You Wish Upon a Star," and a twinge when I hear "Always Let Your Conscience Be Your Guide." In any event, my adventure had begun.

Chapter 4

One father is more than a hundred schoolmasters.
George Herbert

There I lay, staring straight up through the cherry tree at a cloudless summer sky, nestled in sweet-smelling clover with gentle honey bees, their work interrupted, buzzing about my head. Wordsworth would have loved it—except for the blood, and that other buzzing, the one inside my head as I slowly regained consciousness.

It was a couple of months shy of my fourth birthday, and I was allowed to play in the backyard by myself. The gate to the outside world was locked and, except for an occasional look-see by my mother from the third floor railing, I was largely unsupervised. She still had my eighteen-month-old brother to tend to and felt relatively sure that I was safe from harm.

About that blood. I had found two empty orange crates under the house, dragged them to a spot beneath the cherry tree and placed them on end. I laid a small board across the top of the crates, then climbed the thick "Y" shaped trunk to a spot where I could step onto the board. Then, for reasons that only a kid's mind could conjure up, I jumped down to the lawn—backwards. What I hadn't calculated was that the board was higher than I was tall. I caught my chin on the way down. When I rejoined the world of the living, I saw the blood and ran upstairs where I was greeted by the opening theme of radio soap opera *The Romance of Helen Trent* as well as my mother's shrieks. It was a deep cut that required stitches, but that was out of the question. She didn't drive and there was no other quick way to the hospital.

Taking immediate first-aid measures, she cleaned the wound and then reached for an antiseptic. Our medicine cabinet always contained Mercurochrome, iodine and Merthiolate. I don't know why we had the first two because the medical logic in our household always ran along the lines of, "If it burns beyond the limits of human endurance, it must be doing a good job of leaving a wound germ-free." She reached for the Merthiolate. It was my first experience with this potion, apparently popular among sadistic parents. Those who haven't experienced this are probably smiling now. Those who have are more likely gritting their teeth as they suppress a scream that some say can be heard up to six miles on a clear night. Mom applied the Merthiolate; I howled. She then fashioned a chinstrap of gauze and tape. I looked like a tiny football player minus the helmet. I didn't get much sympathy. That wasn't my mother. I did get a stern but brief lecture about being careful, along with a scar I carried for some fifty years before Mother Nature mercifully erased it. She has, however, never erased the memory of the first of my pre-school lessons.

Actually, the term pre-school didn't even exist then, though a few kids went to nursery school. We did not have the "benefit" of play-dates, or *Miss Frances and Ding Dong School*. Not even a conjunction junction (what's your function?) or *Sesame Street*. My pre-school life began with some observations and experimentation in the backyard, as well as some informal academic lessons from my mother and father. All of my surroundings offered opportunities to learn. Among the most vivid of my memories was my dad's love of trains, a fascination that we both shared throughout his life. There is a romance, energy and excitement about them that stirs a sense of drama in most of us. Where are they coming from; where are they going?

He often took me to Waterbury's railroad station. It was a large red brick building capped by a 245-foot clock tower modeled after one in Siena, Italy and still remains the city's primary landmark. The high vaulted ceiling of the main waiting room echoed with the footsteps of travelers and the occasional announcements of arrivals and departures. But the real excitement was out by the platform next to several rows of gleaming tracks, where the mighty steam engines that carried passengers and freight to all parts of the northeast stood, motionless creatures of cast iron. While one engine was quietly breathing alongside the platform, my father lifted me to the engineer's waiting arms so I could sit in the cab. I was thrilled beyond what few words I knew—until the fireman opened the fire door to stoke the boiler with a shovel full of coal. The sudden and unexpected burst of heat and flame gave me such a start that I conked my head on one of the several levers that surrounded me. I began to cry. The engineer quickly handed me back to my dad. The whistle sounded and this wonderful beast that had been quietly snoozing a moment before came to life. It hissed and chugged as huge puffs of cotton-white smoke gushed from the smokestack. Its white-rimmed wheels momentarily slipped, gained traction, then it slowly moved out. The cars passed. I waved to the conductor standing at the back of the caboose. He waved back.

Sadly, these amazing machines would soon be replaced by diesels. They were just not the same, though some were sleek and beautiful. One was called The Blue Goose. It was a super liner that would occasionally visit. We saw it once. I felt the wind on my face as it roared through on the express track. Even then one could sense that it was more than a train. It was a harbinger of post-war America's headlong rush toward a new future filled with technology we couldn't begin to imagine. I later realized that we sometimes have to trade a little romance for technological progress. Still, I'm not so sure that's always a good deal.

On other occasions Dad and I abandoned the urban world and visited the nearby countryside. Connecticut was (and still is) more than seventy-five percent woodlands, and there were plenty of opportunities to stop by one of the many dairy farms in nearby Bethlehem. We often walked to where the cows gathered by the fence under the shade of a maple tree. I remember my amazement at how big they were. I petted one on the nose, and she licked my hand with a tongue long enough to moisten an entire sheet of stamps in one shot. My father indicated the cow's udder and explained its function. He also couldn't resist the opportunity to point out that if the cow couldn't produce any milk it would be an "udder" failure. He cackled. "That's a joke, son." I didn't get it, and I didn't yet know who Senator Foghorn Claghorn was, either.

A few months later, when I began school, the milk break became part of our daily routine. As a five year old I was convinced that to get chocolate milk from a cow, surgeons would open the udder and pour in a chocolate powder (which is what I saw my mother use) to make it. I even envisioned a cow lying on her back as the doctors performed the surgery. It never occurred to me that this really wasn't a necessary step. I mention this only because it demonstrates the bizarre twists a kid's reasoning can take. No matter. I figured the whole thing out by the time I was seventeen. My parents gave me countless hands-on or at least up-close-and-personal- experiences with the world outside our home. Though my Disney Worlds, Lake Quassapaug in Middlebury, Lake Compounce in Bristol, and Savin Rock Amusement Park in West Haven, were great fun, it was the simple experiences that were invaluable in both feeding and satisfying my curiosity, the same kind of curiosity that develops in every kid unless it isn't nurtured at home.

*****

Meanwhile, in the backyard, Patty, a girl about a year older who lived on the second floor, asked me if I'd like to play doctor. I went along with it until I figured out what she meant. I quickly cancelled that appointment. My curiosity was tweaked, however. A few months later I did open a limited, two- patient medical practice of my own. My examinations confirmed that the "plumbing" was indeed different. No big deal. I went back to the sandbox where I continued to construct mountains and tunnels with my bulldozer and steam shovel.

In the winter I further honed my construction skills by building snowmen and igloos. I would fill a soda crate with snow and, with my dad's guidance and muscle, would stack the blocks against a hill until we had a reasonable facsimile of a real igloo. My friend, Mikey Bombadier, would sit inside with me until our teeth chattered.

I should take a moment to note that nature goes about its business quietly in southern New England. Though we have had encounters with tornadoes, hurricanes, floods, and even a few tremors, they are rare. The leaves quietly change colors, the snow silently piles up outside the door, and the buds magically become flowers one May morning. For us Connecticut Yankees, the raw power and fury of nature reveals itself most often in our thunderstorms. Knowing that most children have a natural fear of the flashing and booming, my father would sit me in his lap as a storm was brewing. Our top floor venue provided a spectacular panoramic view of the sky. He explained what was happening because he didn't want me to fear nature's power, but he did want me to have a healthy respect for it. And he wanted me to see its beauty.

He tried to explain that if the crash of thunder came about five seconds after the flash, the lightning had struck about a mile away. We would count to five together. As I later learned, that method of calculation is pretty accurate, though at that time I had no idea what a mile was. There was much to be seen from our veranda. I often watched Mrs. Fasano, an elderly widow who lived next door. She wore the mandatory all-black that older Italian women always seemed to wear and would occasionally chop wood for her stove. I thought only men chopped wood. She was a tough old woman who didn't act according to a role given her by society. She stoically did the work she needed to do. Of course I couldn't articulate those thoughts, and I was confused and a little frightened by her. She looked like an Italian Mammy Yokum, minus the pipe, and seemed pretty fearsome. When I finally worked up the courage to go over to the wire fence to watch her, she was surprisingly pleasant to me. She would smile a toothless smile and pinch my cheek. I knew old people were different. We kids were perfect—no wrinkles, no odors. But I never found the many elderly in our neighborhood repulsive. I was taught to treat them with the utmost respect, mostly through my parents' example, they themselves only in their thirties.

My pre-school academic experience began at our kitchen table. My father took the role of mentor. It was an intuitive thing with him. He later told me he didn't plan or calculate his teaching. He instinctively felt I should know a little about the world I was born into, an advantage he didn't have. Knowing him as I now do, I'm sure he got immeasurable joy from sharing his learning and curiosity with me. My mother, however, had neither the inclination nor the patience to teach, though she actually did so by example. She was never without a book in her lap, and she held education dear. She was one of a very bright group of eight siblings, one of whom went to Harvard and Tufts Medical School and another who attended Bentley, no small accomplishment for an Italian Catholic in the 1920s in what were essentially WASP strongholds. Though my mother rarely read to me, if I had a question, as an avid reader of fiction and non-fiction, she usually had an answer.

My actual academic experience began when my dad handed me a tiny notebook with a red leatherette cover. He announced that this would be my workbook. He gave me a yellow pencil stub (he always kept a ready supply—thousands it seemed), showed me how to hold it and how to make the number one. He asked me to make a bunch of ones—about a page's worth—in my little book and show him what I had done when he returned from work the next day. Satisfied, we went on to two and finally all the way to twenty. He used marbles from our Chinese Checkers set to demonstrate how the number I wrote correlated with the number of things it represented. We repeated the writing drill by printing the alphabet, one letter at a sitting, all in upper case letters. I loved doing it because he couldn't hide his pride when he asked to see my day's work. I was pleased because he was pleased.

The work never became drudgery because of his method. Our little lessons were somewhat irregular, and sometimes we would only review what I had done before, using my little notebook as the starting point. I didn't know why this first taste of learning was important, but his interest was enough of a signal for me to figure out that I should learn these lessons.

Much of this was reinforced by the few books I had, and, I might add, that's all a young kid needs, a few—as long as they're the right ones. I had two illustrated alphabet books (A is for alligator, Z is for zebra), a book of Mother Goose rhymes, and my favorite book of all, *The Lively Little Rabbit*. It was a Little Golden

Book that dealt with the plight of a rabbit who constantly had to be on the watch for a predatory weasel. He, along with a couple of other bunnies and an owl, created a fearsome dragon by using their own bodies as well as some critically placed leaves and twigs. The sight of such a creature terrorized the weasel so much that the other animals were finally able to live in peace. Although the story was read to me (I would look at the illustrations as we moved along), it was the image of that dragon that I never forgot and, by sheer coincidence, was an image familiar to my wife as well, as I discovered more than fifty years after my first encounter with the book. In fact, I was able to find a copy, originally published in 1943, and gave it to my wife for her fifty-eighth birthday. What is interesting about all this is how a simple but powerful image from a children's book can become so deeply etched in a kid's mind, and how that image can set off a whole string of thoughts. Books can do this. TV can't.

Most of what I learned in my pre-school years was more sensed than realized; that is, I really wasn't conscious of what I was absorbing. Surely, I learned a little about being careful, but even that was limited to the confines of our house and yard. What did subtly penetrate was that I was not prince of the castle. Unlike some of today's parents, where one or both seem married to their children, it was clearly evident in our house that my parents were married to each other. I felt sure that I was an integral part of the family, but I had a clearly defined place in that family. For instance, early on I learned I wasn't allowed to interrupt. (I am always both amused and confused when a child interrupts the parent who is engaged in conversation and is then told, "Bobby, how often have I told you not to interrupt? Now what is it?"). I was expected to defer to adults, eat what was on my plate, and say "thank you" and "you're welcome." And never to whine. In short, do as I was told.

My pre-school experiences prepared me to leave the security of my home and, for the first time in my life, deal with adults who were not part of my family, but who had pretty much the same authority over me that my family did. Shortly after my first encounter with school, I would be allowed into the streets to mingle with all the other kids in the neighborhood where I learned many important lessons of a different kind. Because our parents were not intent on making a perfect world for us, life and learning became bigger and more complex. And most of it was still exciting and fun.

Chapter 5

Education is hanging around until you've caught on ...

Robert Frost

It was September 1947, the Wednesday after Labor Day, the traditional first day of school in these parts. Our threesome toddled out the front door and walked toward Dikeman Street, which spilled out onto Wood Street just opposite our place. Mom wore a smart bankers'-gray suit and a black velvet beret. I had on my sailor suit, authentic in every detail down to my Chief Petty Officer's insignia. My father's cousin, Al Gioielli, a tailor by trade, had created it during the war while on duty aboard the aircraft carrier Lexington (and later opened a tailor shop of the same name in Manchester, Connecticut).

Together my mother and I pushed my brother Al's stroller toward Walsh Grammar School, no more than five hundred feet from our front door. When we arrived, the principal, Mr. Buckman, greeted us and directed us to my kindergarten classroom down the hall where my life would take on a new dimension, actually a second dimension, one quite different from my life at home.

We waited as Miss Keenan met other parents and children. When our turn came, she and Mom exchanged social niceties. Mom introduced me, gave me a kiss on the cheek and two parting words: "Behave yourself." Miss Keenan was somewhere in her mid-fifties, gray-haired and slightly middle-aged plump. She was possessed of a sweet and gentle manner but was clearly in charge, a veteran who knew her job and how to handle kids. This gave her a decided edge over her younger colleagues, and though she couldn't have possibly known it then, she had an even greater advantage over today's teachers. Like Opie's Aunt Bea, she had warmth, wisdom, and patience, as well as a gentle and polite tenacity. But she had one more important thing that all teachers should have, namely us, a class of kids ready and eager to learn. We came from homes where parents usually instilled in us, at the very least, a semblance of good behavior.

When I was about thirteen, I remember reading an article in Reader's Digest about a woman in New Mexico who used to take in troubled kids and work with them on her ranch. She said, "Kids are like horses; you don't teach them, you train them." Today this remark would undoubtedly bring gasps from certain quarters. Kids are like horses? What would that do for their self-esteem? The fact is our parents did train us. They trained us to practice some self-restraint, to be respectful toward others, especially adults, to be reasonably responsible for our actions, and to expect unpleasant consequences when we stepped out of line. The training was reinforced by all adults in our lives—aunts, uncles, neighbors, teachers, clergy, even store clerks. Strange thing is, I don't remember anybody saying much about behavior per se. Despite our tender years, we sensed what they expected and, for the most part, complied. What was made abundantly clear was that disruption and interruption were absolutely unacceptable.

Those matters already taken care of, Miss Keenan could concentrate on her job as a teacher. We learned our letters and numbers; we placed differently shaped blocks of wood into the proper spaces; we gained a little hand-eye coordination by coloring with oversized crayons, we sang to Miss Keenan's piano playing, and even were allowed to accompany her on some simple instruments. I wowed my classmates with my skill on the triangle. Speaking of "wow," a very pretty girl named Eileen, with shoulder-length chestnut curls and dressed in dark-green velvet, saw me struggling with loose shoelaces and taught me how to tie them. And so it was that we learned from each other, as well as Miss Keenan, whose gentle nudges painlessly prepared us for more formal academic exercises. We were being trained to be students.

Though kindergarten life was a protected reality, unfortunately, the outside world found a way to poke its head into the picture. My life was no exception. Twice during my first year in school I was visited by the real world in the form of serious illness and death.

In October my paternal grandmother died. I often visited her for a chat every now and then in her small apartment attached to the first floor of our house. She was a robust woman whose energy filled the room. She sometimes pinched my cheek so hard that I would later stand on the toilet seat to check in the mirror to see if my face had become permanently disfigured. She affectionately called me *stunod* (I don't think that needs any translation). Unfortunately, just as I was beginning to know her, her energy waned and she became ill. I remember the red and white Cadillac ambulance backing into the driveway and my granny being taken out of her apartment on a gurney. She died a few days later.

I asked my dad why she hadn't returned. He explained that she went to live with God in heaven. I accepted that, but still there was a hole in my little world that I really didn't understand. Why did she have to go live with God? My father further explained that when we get very old our body dies but our spirit goes to heaven. The question of why still stuck in my head, but time took care of it, I think.

In retrospect, my dad handled the situation correctly. Today's parents have been guilted, bamboozled, and pressured by a cadre of mental health professionals into thinking that they must go into agonizing detail at great length about any human tragedy, be it on a national or personal scale. This neither toughens kids nor does it make them more sensitive to the human condition. There is no need to heap upon them detailed knowledge of life's misery. Soon enough they will come to know of these things. The situation should be simply and clearly explained and the child then should go on being a child. Time will heal their hurt, and time will bring them to a greater understanding of life's darker side. Today many adults seem to think kids are super-sensitive creatures who need to be taught how to grieve. They are wrong. Children's worlds are solipsistically limited largely to how they are affected by life's vagaries. Kids know only of their own world, and for the most part their sensitivity doesn't run deep or far where others are concerned. That is as it should be. That is the logical starting place from which to learn.   The larger consciousness will come (we hope) with the passing of time. It took me many years to realize how another's gentleness and understanding, and a small and simple good deed, can affect the rest of our lives.

My second visit from reality came with a bout of double pneumonia in the winter of 1947–1948. My mother often watched me walk down Dikeman Street toward home from her third-floor perch in the living room window. Until the day she died, she insisted I got sick because I had not buttoned my jacket against the cold winter air. She and my father had the unnerving habit of blaming me for every illness I contracted (with the exception of mumps, measles, and chicken pox). That kind of irrational response to a child's illness could be the stuff of a good psychological study, but I won't go down that path. I learned to simply brush off some of their beliefs, which were probably rooted in a combination of their own upbringing and homemade diagnoses, which, in turn, sprang from decades of limited medical knowledge and ignorance concerning bacteria and viruses.

In any event I grew worse, and with the snow piling up outside, my father carried me down the winding staircase of the dark and rarely used front hallway. I was taken to St. Mary's Hospital where I would spend the next five days.

I wasn't afraid of being alone, but I quickly developed a fear of the staff and the periodic penicillin shots they had to administer. Some of my nurses were nuns garbed in habits of flowing white. These angels of no mercy would silently float into my room and hover to administer my scheduled penicillin injection. I kicked and screamed with all my might as two held me down and another pushed that needle so deep into my bottom that I thought it would come out the other side and stick into the mattress. Six times a day they and I would endure this contest, which, of course, I always lost.

On about the third day a lovely, honey-voiced young nun came to my bedside unaccompanied by the usual mistresses of torture. She explained that if I promised to relax as she held my hand and rubbed my arm when I got my "medicine," I would feel no pain, only a little mosquito bite. To my amazement, that's exactly what happened.

Some adults tended to be a little too tough on our generation, partly because of any older generation's tendency to muscle the younger one, but also because some of those who had weathered the Depression and the war had developed a toughness that bordered on callousness. Add that to nuns who had experienced the rigid discipline of the church and who, of course, had no children of their own, and it isn't difficult to see how some became hardened. They insisted on pounding the square peg into the round hole. Fortunately, the thought of using a little more flexibility in dealing with kids was developing and that wonderful nun's sensitive and caring approach eliminated my fear of needles from that point on. I'm sure I would have gotten past the kicking and screaming by the time I was thirty-five or so, but the worst part of any medical procedure is that shuddering anticipation, that quaking fear in our bowels that the thought of pain can bring on. Her tenderness took away the pain as well as the fear. She made it clear that I was going to have to get the injection, but I had choices in the way I was going to accept it. She taught me a good early-life lesson. Offering a kid, actually anyone, firm and realistic options is not a bad way to go. Little did I realize that these two brushes with the realities of pain and death were only the beginning.

When I returned to school and resumed my walks home, I often took minor detours into backyards or over to Putnam Street just off my normal route along Dikeman Street. Curiosity made what was usually a five-minute trip into a mini-journey of a half hour or more. My mother's nervousness finally submitted to the reality that her little boy was learning more about the world beyond his backyard and the schoolyard. In any event, my life was about to gain an all-important third dimension, one of further independence, responsibility, and risk. I had reached the point where a very young, very small person started to deal with becoming a whole person.

Chapter 6

It takes all sorts of in and outdoor schooling . . .
Robert Frost

The pace of life began to pick up as kindergarten quietly moved toward a June finale, which was more of a whimper than a bang. We were pointed in the direction of first grade without any pretentious graduation ceremony such as those now in vogue in some schools which are not conducted for kids; rather, they are designed to pander to parents; to feed them the illusion of achievement. Sadly, we have become a society enamored of these phony symbols of merit and nowhere more than in our schools.

My daily walks to and from school proved to be safe and uneventful, and it was still a few decades before the Fretful Mothers' Club of America would be chartered. So, as the late spring days grew warmer and lengthened, my mother mustered the courage to release me from my backyard stockade. Of course, I must admit, the risk involved in allowing a five-year-old to venture from the house then was minimal compared to that of today. My parents knew the neighbors, many of whom I would soon come to regard as surrogate parents. The streets were much quieter. Virtually every family owned only one car, and that was gone from about 6:30 am to 3:30 pm when the factories let out. Some folks didn't even own a car and simply walked to work or rode one of Waterbury's three bus lines. It was a short walk from our house on Wood Street to a bus stop on Walnut or East Farms Street. Our neighborhood saw little commercial traffic during the day, and the narrow streets forced any vehicles that came along to move at much slower speeds than we are now accustomed to. Drivers were well aware that in an urban setting the streets were our playground.

I was cautioned to stay on the sidewalk on our side of the street, but that didn't last too long. At first, I rarely ventured very far from our home. Five or six houses was my self-imposed limit, and all that was needed to find playmates. Playing with other kids was fun, but at that age playmates generally aren't interesting. What was interesting was that street life gave me contact with real adults. Certainly parents and teachers were adults, but I tended to see them only in terms of their roles. I was shocked whenever I saw teachers at a grocery store or in church. It was as if I didn't expect them to eat or worship or to have any kind of life beyond school. As well as a five-year-old can, I was able to see a bit of the human dimensions in the neighborhood's working adults I encountered near my home. I wasn't blinded from seeing their humanity as I was by the kind of authoritative relationship I had with my parents and teachers.

What was most interesting about my newfound liberation was that, in a small but significant way, I got to see people at work. I saw my teachers at work, but I was part of their work process so I couldn't separate myself from that. Some of those workers I saw in the streets were soon to disappear from American life. Times were changing fast as America flexed its post-war manufacturing muscle, and technology edged some jobs into little more than a remembrance of simpler times. A perceptive adult could see the near future, but as a little kid, I was still able to see a bit of the past.

I could hear that distant but familiar nasal cry from one hundred yards away where Vine turned into Wood Street. He sounded like a Canada goose stuck in second gear. I ran up all three flights of the back stairs as fast as I could and burst into the kitchen as the banjos on the radio strummed "I'm Looking Over a Four Leaf Clover," one of my favorites. My mother was cutting green beans at her usual station at the sink. I breathlessly begged for any old cloths she had as well as an apple cut into a few slices. She always co-operated with these requests. She knew how fascinated I was with the ragman.

She handed me a few of my brother's old diapers and an apple cut into quarters. I raced back down the stairs. I could hear the clip-clopping of his tired old horse, straining against the steep grade with the flatbed wagon in tow. "Raaaags," the bearded old timer called out, and there I was with a handful of them.

Actually it was a trade-off. He got the rags (which, as I understand it, would be sold to paper manufacturers for a pittance), and I got to feed his horse, which he told me was named Pete. I asked permission, then moved cautiously forward. Old Pete would lower his head. He was scarred and badly in need of grooming, his mane scruffy and snarled. I petted his nose, always amazed to find that horses had whiskers. With my other hand palm up, I offered him a slice of apple. It tickled as those large square teeth and curling lips took it from my hand. I produced the rest of the apple from my pocket and continued to pet him with the other hand. His sad eyes didn't change though, and I began to feel sorry for this creature that worked so hard to get so little, pretty much like his owner. As he moved on, Pete's horseshoes left an imprint in the soft summer asphalt.

The ragman was only one part of the continuous parade of adults who moved in and out of my life by simply doing their jobs. The iceman didn't have a horse and wagon, but it was interesting to watch him grab a huge block of ice in his tongs and head off to refill someone's icebox. The people on the top floors would place signs in their windows that simply read "ICE" in huge block letters. We, however, had graduated to a Westinghouse with a freezer the size of a glove compartment which, amazingly, still purrs away in my dad's basement some fifty-five years later. Quite a testament to American workmanship in those days. Just as the brand name Kleenex was synonymous with tissues, in our house the term "Frigidaire" was applied to any refrigerator. In fact, when we moved two years later, our new kitchen range was a Frigidaire. Talk about really confusing a little kid. The man who delivered our refrigerator in the summer of 1948 had, unbelievably, strapped it to his back and climbed the three flights at the rear of our home to bring it in the back door. Mom was thrilled, but for me it was no longer the same as my friend the iceman. He always gave me shards of ice to suck on and keep me cool on a hot summer day. A poor man's Popsicle.

The fruit and vegetable man drove a converted surplus army bus still sporting the khaki green that was seemingly ubiquitous then. The mailboxes and mail trucks, simply by virtue of their color, were the most visible remnants of a war now over. The produce man's future was limited, though. He brought the product to the homes of housewives who didn't work or drive. My parents made their weekly Thursday (payday) trip to the A&P, but for those who still had iceboxes and little opportunity to get to the grocery store on a regular basis, or for those with a little greater income, that khaki green bus served a purpose. But times were changing fast and within just a couple of years he went the way of the ragman and iceman.

In the late forties and early fifties, at least here in the East, oil heat became the homeowners' choice. But before we got to our new home, I genuinely looked forward to the coalmen's visit. They carried that beautiful black and shiny anthracite in a large square canvas basket slung over their shoulders, each taking his turn to dump his load as the other returned to the truck for more. When they reached the coal chute that led to the bin in the cellar, they would adroitly flip their coal bucket over their shoulders and into the chute with uncanny accuracy, but a few pieces would always fall to the ground, and I would grab them and carefully examine these black diamonds, then run off to draw crude portraits on the concrete sidewalk behind our house.

In considering future occupations, I was torn between becoming a coal man or a garbage man, maybe because, busy as they were, both took a moment to greet me. I think they saw the admiration in my face. They did their tedious jobs well, with efficiency, and without an attitude. In my own little kid way, I respected them. I still do.

Though I saw sadness in the ragman's horse, it was our street cleaner's face, a cross between circus clown Emmett Kelly and Jackie Gleason's character the Poor Soul, in which I could recognize the sadness of a life lost. Almost six years old, I didn't have the words then, but, as one of my finest college professors, Dr. Milton Stern, told me, "You knew what you knew." Indeed I did.

This laborer was announced by the jingling and clanging of his shovel, dustpan, and brooms, as well as the rattle of the huge iron-spoked wheels of his barrel, as he slowly pushed his way up the street. I can only guess that this man was a down-and-outer who was given something to do so he could sustain himself.

Before the days of the motorized power sweeper, these men could be found in and around the downtown area. Every couple of weeks during the summer our man would appear to sweep the litter-filled cobblestone gutters. Popsicle sticks, bubblegum wrappers, bottle caps, empty cigarette packs, and butts were everywhere. Now, a more mobile society leaves it on the highways.

He never spoke to me—not one word. He looked at me through red-rimmed bloodshot eyes and just grunted if I offered to help. The bulbous, blue-veined nose, unkempt mustache, three-day growth of beard, and saggy jowls composed the face that sat atop a tattered brown tweed suit, which reeked of tobacco. His sartorial choice was always the same, which, of course, meant he had no choice. The summer heat and the bowler he sometimes wore made him perspire profusely, so much so it seemed as if he were perpetually crying—like a tearful Oliver Hardy. I guess the flask he occasionally took from his breast pocket told the story, but then I didn't even know what it held. All I knew was what I saw and it saddened me.

Just a few feet away from where the street cleaner did his work was another workingman who provided a brighter picture. Mike the tailor (Mike Rosa) had a storefront shop in the house next to us, where he lived. His doors were always wide-open in the days before air conditioning, and he allowed little ones to run in and out where we hid behind the racks of suits and dresses during an intensive game of hide-and-seek. As long as we were careful, he never seemed to mind our interruption.

During slower moments in his day and mine, he would let me watch him ply his trade. I was fascinated by the sewing machine. Spinning wheels and the clickety-clack as he pumped the treadle would attract any kid. What was truly mesmerizing was watching him hem a pant cuff or a skirt. His thimbled finger pushed the needle through the material and made a loop so adroitly that it was a continuous motion, faster than the pigeons downtown could pick up popcorn off the pavement. He sat there dressed in a suit jacket, legs crossed, glasses on the end of his nose, and effortlessly altered clothing or created a suit as if he were working from an architect's plan. He had that gift to see it all in his mind before it ever happened. I sensed he was every bit as much the artist as the fellow who played his sax on street corners downtown—only Mike's music was a silent kind.

Three houses up, on the same side of the street as the sweet and gentle tailor, lived our neighborhood child-killer. I suspect many locales spawned similar myths that lingered and sometimes flourished as long as there were the very young to believe them and later pass them on. My greatest fear, in fact my only fear, was Mr. Ritchie.

Monkey see, monkey do, so it didn't take long to learn from those a couple of years older that if we ran up the few wooden steps onto Mr. Ritchie's wide veranda, with only the warm summer air and a screen door between him and us, and jumped up and down to make a fierce racket, we would find ourselves looking squarely into death's maw. So it was in the gloaming of one August evening that I heard the Sirens' call. It was clear and strong. Unlike Ulysses, there was no one to tie me down. The butterflies began to dance in my stomach and my bowels began to quake. Could I? Would I? Something took hold of me and propelled me toward that veranda at near light speed. I answered the challenge to live life on the edge.

The next moment there I was, dancing and jumping, wildly gesticulating like one of Stanley Kubrick's apes in *2001: A Space Odyssey.* I stopped for a second to wait for a reaction. When I looked up, there he was, only inches away on the other side of that screen door. He looked like movie bad guy Edward G. Robinson. He had that same menacing scowl, an ugly grimace frozen for all time. He growled. I opened my mouth to scream but nothing came out. I turned and leapt off the porch with legs already cranking in high gear like a cartoon character in pursuit, only I was the quarry. I hit the pavement laughing and shrieking at the same time, that kind of giddy, fearful scream we let out just as the roller coaster rounds the top of that first gut-wrenching drop.

I looked over my shoulder for my pursuer, but there was none. I had beaten the odds and had already begun to gloat over my invincibility. Fear was no longer part of my vocabulary—or should I say scaredy-cat? Though, I must admit, I never tempted that particular fate again.

Fast-forward about twenty-two years to 1970 and one of those chance meetings to which no odds can apply; one of those delayed learning experiences that demonstrates how inaccurate our childhood perceptions can be. My good friend and teaching colleague, Mike Doyle, and I had played golf at Western Hills in Waterbury one summer day. I needed a haircut and asked if he minded the wait. He surprised me and said he'd get one, too. Impressed by my continued loyalty to a barber whose shop was now twenty miles from my home, he decided to join me. Off we went to the Universal Barber Shop that sat on Bauby's Corner one story up behind huge plate glass windows that overlooked the very center of the city. Pat Giordano, my barber, performed his magic on both of us with his usual warm-hearted wit. Mike was pleased and that pleased me.

Down the stairs and out onto the corner of West Main and South Main, we sprinted across the street to beat the light and stopped right in front of the long stretch of benches that bordered Waterbury's large tree-lined green. It was here that most city buses pulled in to pick up passengers. And suddenly, on that sleepy summer afternoon, I came face to face with someone I had seen only a few times in my early childhood—through a screen door. I recognized Mr. Ritchie instantly. It was a reflexive thing, the kind of thing that happens when you don't think about it, when you don't get in the way of your brain. I stepped toward this small man and began to explain who I was, where I had "met" him. He only smiled as he squinted into the sun. He didn't recognize me, and I don't think he understood much of what I said, though he did recognize the name Gioiella, which was our last name before the spelling was changed in the early forties.

What did register with me was that his was the face of a kind and gentle person. Then it dawned on me. He had never been a monster. He had apparently volunteered to accept a role just to have fun with us, to bring us the kind of screaming joy kids love. It occurred to me that if he didn't enjoy our taunts, all he had to do was ignore us, and we would have given up. Or, worse by far, he could have simply told our parents. Then we would have really faced murder. He relished his bad guy image because we counted on it for a thrill, and it made him a special part of our world if only for a brief moment. Still a bit confused, he smiled and gave me a warm handshake.

Mike and I found my Dodge Dart on the other side of the green and headed back to Bristol. We turned toward Interstate 84, but my mind was on an old wooden veranda on Wood Street just about a mile and a half away. I shudder to think what might have happened to Mr. Ritchie today. Would the Fretful Mothers' Club demand his arrest? Would we need counseling? Would the local news make him the fear-du-jour?

That summer of '48 ended with another encounter with a grump—actually the original Grumpy. I saw *Snow White* that year when Disney re-released its blockbuster. It didn't have the same effect on me that *Pinocchio* did, but for some reason, I particularly liked and always remembered the shadows of the dwarves on the walls of the mine tunnels where they "hi-ho'd." I loved Dopey. I knew I did not like Grumpy, but what I did not know then was that he had an even less pleasant sister, and she was soon to become my first grade teacher.

While the summer of '48 had provided me with some valuable street lessons, the winter of that year taught me a little something about the satisfaction in helping others. In early December we had had a huge snowfall and even trucks were having a tough time on our hill. A local soda bottling company, which produced Diamond Ginger Ale and Pal, a popular non-carbonated orange drink, had apparently sent out its trucks in spite of conditions that bordered on the impossible.

I was playing in our driveway with my tiny aluminum shovel when the soda truck came down Wood Street and parked in a huge snowbank right in front of our house. Having made their delivery to a small variety store across the street, it then took only a moment for the driver and his helper to discover that they were stuck. One of them asked to borrow my shovel. It was no match for a huge mound of frozen snow and bent almost in half with the force the driver applied. The wheels spun, they cursed, I was amused. Then I remembered that my dad always used coal cinders on the sidewalk and often let me help spread them. The driver had already asked if we had any sand. Sensing their frustration, I asked if cinders would help. They were desperate for any solution, so I led them into our basement to a full pail next to the coal furnace. The ashes solved the problem.

My dad wasn't home so these fellows had turned to a six-year-old for help. It was a great feeling, but it didn't match the pride that came from a simple gesture a minute later. As soon as they were free of the snowbank, they stopped. The helper reached into the racks and pulled out a quart bottle (no liters in those days) of Diamond Ginger Ale and a twelve-ounce bottle of kids' favorite non-carbonated orange drink, Pal. He slid each down the snowbank and yelled, "Thanks a lot kid." I was thrilled beyond words. Not because I got free soda (it was probably worth about a quarter), but because I had been compensated for my effort.

I ran upstairs with my rewards. I gave the ginger ale to my mother. The carbonation was too rough for my throat then and even years later. That night at dinner, (which we poor people called supper), I drank the Pal. My dad took the cork liner out of the bottle cap, placed the metal cap on the outside of my shirt and fitted the cork liner into the cap from the inside. The cap announced I was a pal. I couldn't hide my pride and wore it to bed that night.

These were just the beginnings of my street life in the North End. It would last only two more years before we moved to a very different environment in the suburbs, which were still more rural than suburban, but could never have offered the first precious and enriching experiences I had had in an urban setting.

Some things we can help; some we can't. The sterility of today's suburbia is largely the natural result of a society that has moved on, away from a fixed way of life toward a mobility that is both a blessing and a curse. All those vendors who visited our streets have become part of our super grocery stores and malls. The kids who once filled the streets, even in suburban areas, have largely disappeared—inside—to play video games that would make a G.I. cringe, and to watch television shows that have removed almost all sense of propriety and shame from our society.

Maybe empty streets equate with empty lives. I'm not sure.

Chapter 7

Something wicked this way comes.

Macbeth

Who can forget Margaret Hamilton's wonderful characterization of the Wicked Witch of the West in the *Wizard of Oz*? She frightened my boys so much that they ran and cowered behind their grandfather's overstuffed chair when they first saw that classic visage on television. My first encounter with that snarling, evil creature was also on television in the late fifties. I was, of course, too old to be frightened by her then, but had actually met that hatchet face some years earlier—up close and personal in first grade. In fact, whenever Miss Gallen blew into the room, it would not have been altogether unreasonable to expect to see her accompanied by a cadre of flying monkeys.

There was much to be learned in this, my first academic experience, which, as it turned out, offered far more than book learning. Our first mission in school was to learn to read, the most important skill we would ever acquire. We used the traditional *Dick and Jane* series with its engrossing story lines: "Look Jane, look. See Spot run. See the car. Look out Spot. Oohh . . ." A real page-turner. Actually the illustrations were more interesting to me because I was envious of Dick and Jane's lovely Cape Cod style home, white picket fence and all. Their grandparents also played a role in their lives. Three of mine were gone, and I rarely saw the sole survivor, my maternal grandmother, who lived with us a couple of years later for what proved to be her last year of life. She spoke little English and didn't relate well to my brother or me. No warm fuzzies there I'm sad to say.

I saw my life as somewhat lacking compared to that of my blond-haired, blue-eyed friends, Dick and Jane. I didn't even have a Spot. All we had was a stray cat named Stinky who responded only to my father and would never come into our house. No wonder. She too had probably read *Dick and Jane*.

I don't remember more than that about my formal learning experience that year, except that Miss Gallen would periodically call me to the corner near her desk and sit me on a stool in front of an easel which held a super-enlarged version of our *Dick and Jane* textbook. She would then whip her sword out of her scabbard, actually I think it was her pointer, and indicate which lines she wanted me to read.

Kids got report cards then that had letter grades on them, even in the first grade. Many school districts today don't use letter grades for the primary years opting instead to use written comments to inform parents of a student's progress. This can be effective and less stigmatizing if done properly. It can also be misused and misleading if political correctness doesn't allow for an honest evaluation. One superintendent in the system in which I taught insisted that no negative comments appear on the report card. Often the truth took a back seat to schmoozing Mom and Dad. I assume those one-on-one sessions on the stool were Miss Gallen's way of assessing our progress and, therefore, the basis for our grades which ranged from A to P (for poor).

In retrospect, I don't remember much about actually learning to read. I do remember that I identified many words using the "see and say" method, i.e., I had apparently memorized words and later recalled them from rote memory—what teachers called "sight vocabulary." We also used phonics to sound out those words that we did not recognize. And we drilled and drilled and drilled. The combination of all these, especially the constant drilling, tedious for the teacher but critical for the student, led to our learning the most important skill any of us ever learns in school.

That was a good thing. What I'm not sure of is the degree to which our fear of Miss Gallen contributed to or detracted from our learning that year. I'm a big fan of fear's place in the classroom—used prudently and reasonably. Though we all tended to fear our teachers to a greater or lesser degree, it was the fear of shaming or disappointing our parents that was most effective. It kept us in line and served as one important kind of motivator. But our fear of Miss Gallen was completely disproportionate to the classroom experience, and with good reason. She left a wrinkle in our school year that we would all remember. I suppose most youngsters are resilient enough to survive someone like her.   But one student almost didn't.

His name was Vincent. He was the only first-grade classmate I remember for three reasons: He sat next to me; he dressed like no other student I have seen before or since; and he became the victim of cruelty that almost defies explanation.

He was quiet. Head down, he always remained (as they say in the education business) on task. What would have made him an anomaly in almost any public school classroom, then or now, was his sartorial splendor. He wore suits, sometimes even vested, virtually every day. Even in the hot weather he would wear a shirt and tie. My best guess is that he was the child of post-war immigrants who placed education next to godliness (now there's a thought), and/or whose father was a tailor. In any event, in a world that now considers a new pair of Nikes and clean sweats semi-formal dress, he would probably suffer a daily fate in the schoolyard that I would rather not think about. On second thought, he would have probably preferred to suffer that fate rather than the one the cruel gods, through their faithful minion Miss Gallen, had visited upon him one day about a couple of months into the fall semester.

As I casually glanced over to my left, I caught what I thought was a reflection of some sort beneath Vincent's desk. Though it was the first time I had encountered this not completely unheard of occurrence (at least in the very early grades), it didn't take me long to figure out that that reflection was a growing puddle of urine. Poor Vincent had peed his pants. I sat mortified and immediately felt his shame. What could or should I do? Vincent sat there, frozen in fear. It wasn't long before there were a couple of ooh's and aah's and then, like a cat awaiting the slightest movement in the brush, Miss Gallen leapt upon her prey.

That moment brings to mind the cold war inspired air-raid drills of the late forties and early fifties—"Duck and Cover" they were called. At our teacher's signal, we would slip beneath our desks, curl up in a ball, and kiss our fannies good-bye. That pretty much describes what happened that day. The room sat as if in suspended animation. The fuse had been lit.

Before I could melt into the varnished floor beneath my desk, she was there—her face in his face. Then came the explosion, the simultaneous shock wave, and the ensuing silence. A small mushroom cloud rose above her head, one of the monkeys coughed, and then came the nuclear wind. She hit Vincent with a torrent of venom, ugly words that stripped him of what little, if any, dignity he had left. We all sat in mortal fear, but there were no nervous chuckles. Vincent was one of us. As she wildly gesticulated with her hands, all of us knew Miss Gallen had overstepped the bounds of human decency. And then, as quickly as it happened, he was gone. The seat was empty, and the janitor was tending to the puddle.

Vincent came back the next day; so did Miss Gallen. It would become clear that events of the previous day had left an aftertaste that would linger for the remainder of the year. But it appeared that Miss Gallen had changed her tone. She wasn't exactly contrite, but it seemed as if someone had gotten to her, or maybe she had gotten to herself. We were too young to fully appreciate the change and, even if we had, the fear of her fury still set the tenor of the class.

Looking back, I now realize that all this heat produced some light. Surely a severe reprimand, a full apology to Vincent and the class, and a stern administrative warning were in order. But there is much more to this than meets the eye, and it would probably apply to all the Miss Gallens we endured. There is no question that some awfully mean people get into the classroom. But even those of a more temperate nature can sometimes be turned off and become permanently bitter about their fate. Such was probably true of many of the women who taught us all those years ago. In Connecticut female teachers (and some librarians) were not allowed to marry until 1940. Add to that the fact that women, even in the years beyond the forties, had about three career choices: teacher, nurse, or secretary. Those with even less training could become store clerks or factory workers. For those who began to teach fifteen or twenty years before 1940, though they were still young, their fate was pretty much sealed, and we can be sure more than a few thought about that as they packed up their papers and books to head home for the evening. The meager pay, as well as the limited and somewhat restricted social life, led to their being trapped. Many never escaped the homes and families in which they grew up. Their lives were confined to a classroom filled with kids, and no matter how cute and well-behaved those children might have been, that environment can be taxing, even for the most loving soul.

Miss Gallen was mean but not incompetent. We still went on to learn to read. And, in spite of Vincent's humiliation, even this ugly incident had a plus side. We learned survival techniques. As we all eventually found out, virtually none of our teachers were pushovers. All, even those who had some humor or gentleness, had a no-nonsense attitude toward the actual learning process. Fooling around would usually bring a reprimand from any one of them.

We also learned to take care of teacher-student conflicts ourselves. For most of us, there was little other choice. Kids will complain only if they think they have a listening ear. Most of us didn't, and generally that's a good thing. If a child thinks he has found an ally in his parents about a teacher-related gripe, it can eventually hurt him. Kids can quickly develop an "attitude" if parents have even subtly implied the teacher is wrong (even though that may be the case). The child will carry that attitude from teacher to teacher, a posture that can divert the kid's focus from where it should be—on learning. I have witnessed this more than once. If a moan or a whine did sneak through, most parents responded as mine did: "Just behave yourself and do your work." They didn't go through some thought process prescribed by the latest talk-show guru. Their response was instinctive. They felt that school was our responsibility. Except in extreme cases, the problems were ours to resolve. They were trying to get on with their lives and had not yet been told by a gaggle of new-wave psychologists that they must devote every waking minute to their children's needs and feelings. I don't think their inaction resulted in a generation of psychologically challenged children. This is not to imply that we could or should suffer continuous emotional drubbings from the Miss Gallens of the world, but that notwithstanding, in the long run we all probably benefited from a tussle with a toughie—and moved on.

*****

Second grade was enjoyable for several reasons, not the least of which was Miss Kilroy. She was older and had a get-the-job-done approach, but she liked us. She was a pro.

We also found ourselves part of something new in education at that time: two to a desk, a girl and a boy. Our brand new movable desks of gray tubing and formica tops went beyond their utilitarian value. After a couple of years of the classroom routine, little boys can get frisky, as veteran primary grade teachers have told me. By having a young lady as a seatmate, we boys were gently pushed toward staying on course and addressing the subject of the moment. It was a learn-by-example experiment. Girls are much more mature at that age. They stick to the task and are far less prone to goof around. My savior was named Paula. She had brown, straight, shoulder-length hair with bangs, large square teeth, full lips, and a warm smile. Actually it was confusing at that age. Was I supposed to like Paula? Had some strange karma thrown us together? Sadly, I do not remember her last name, but I do remember that she was a very nice girl who kept me focused and provided some relief from classroom tedium.

We continued to do essentially the same things we did in first grade except we took the lessons up a notch. Nothing new was dragged into the curriculum simply because it was assumed we had sufficiently mastered a particular skill. The thought then was that kids needed continuous training in the basics. That meant repetition. Those drills we went through, from an adult perspective, now seem mind-numbing, and for an adult they would be. But for kids it's really a painless and productive process. Proof? Look at us—those of us who lived that experience. Did we not learn our three R's thoroughly and with ease? We weren't being taught for a test that some government or educational bureaucrat decided would be the final measure of our classroom progress. Ironically, it is those who successfully learned from methods used in the thirties, forties, fifties and sixties who have fallen prey to the whole super-test mentality that has spread like a cancer from local and state to federal levels. Teaching for such tests leads to educational chaos and less content learning for the kids. Veteran classroom teachers know this well, but sadly have only just begun to raise their voices in unison. I shudder to think how all the Miss Kilroys would react.

Actually, second grade was not an unpleasant experience for all the right reasons. Things moved along as they were supposed to. From a personal level, I recall few moments of distress. In fact, only one memory of that kind lingers, and it reflects more upon my over-reaction to a not very serious passing remark that Miss Kilroy could never have guessed would cost me an entire day of learning.

We had just returned from Christmas vacation when she announced that we could bring in a toy to play with the next day because, for some unexplained reason, we would not be going outside for recess. I was just moving into my cowboy mode at that point, so I naturally decided to bring my new set of Roy Rogers six-shooters for the next day's recess. I had been faithfully listening to *Bobby Benson and the B-Bar-B Riders* (he would yell "Bee-Bar-Bee" at the outset of every adventure) and was clearly inspired by this seven-or-eight-year-old kid who led an entire ranch—a whole posse of adult cowboys. The thought of such an arrangement was absurd, but the premise seemed perfectly logical to me.

The next morning I strapped on the six guns that my cousin Sonny (Guy Colella) and his beautiful bride Bernie had given me for Christmas. I wore them under my green winter coat, so they had not been noticed before I stuffed them in my desk in anticipation of a great indoor recess. The clock approached 2:15, afternoon recess time, and I began to reach into my desk. As I caressed my six-shooters, Miss Kilroy got off a shot of her own. "I will not allow anyone to play with guns at recess. If anyone brought guns, I will take them and give them to the janitor to toss into the furnace."

I think I went into cardiac arrest. I almost had a "Vincent" moment. My seatmate, Paula, looked at me strangely, her large square teeth more frightening than usual. How could Miss Kilroy do this, I thought. Why didn't she tell us there was a no-gun policy before that day? There I was on the brink of developing a potential career as a cowboy, and she shattered my dreams with an ex post facto blast below the gun belt.

I left my guns in my desk and let the rest of the day's lessons drift by as I focused on an image of those smooth faux-ivory handles spinning end over end into the furnace's flaming maw. As I noted earlier, I took things seriously. At the end of the school day, after I had gone to the cloak room (we had no lockers) and returned with my winter coat already on, I furtively took the gun belt out of the desk and strapped it around my chest. With a six-gun under each arm, I walked out of the room looking like a mini-Charles Atlas.

My ambitions suffered another albeit less serious blow a few weeks later. As part of my cowpoke-in-training regimen, I listened to every Western I could between 5:00 and 7:30 pm, my usual bedtime in second grade—if I were good. I sat in the kitchen and listened to the radio that sat on top of the refrigerator as my mother prepared our dinner. At 5:00 there was *Tom Mix* presented by Instant Ralston, and at 5:15 *Sergeant Preston of the Royal Canadian Mounties* and his faithful dog King ("On King, on you huskies!") presented by Quaker Puffed Wheat and Puffed Rice ("Shot from real guns"). I never figured out how, never mind why, they did that. I loved both shows, but Tom Mix had the edge because he was a cowboy. He had a horse named Tony. This confused me because I had heard my mother speak of Toni home permanents (there's a memorable smell), and I had an Uncle Tony. I just couldn't figure out how a horse could be named Tony, but then of course there had been Pete, the ragman's horse, so I accepted it.

One of Tom's adventures offered an interesting example of a *deus ex machina* and, better yet, offered me a chance to participate in it, even if it was after the fact. The scenario wasn't plausible, but it worked for me. Tom was trapped in a cave by a couple of bad guys. Unable to shoot his way out, he got an idea. He just happened to have two rings (why two?) with a topaz stone in each. He placed the two on a stick a few inches apart. The outlaws saw the yellow reflections and thought they were about to encounter a mountain lion. They fled; Tom was saved. But more important, we, the listeners, could have one or more of the very same rings that saved Tom. A box top from any Ralston Purina product would do it. No problem there. I loved Wheat Chex and still do, though I did backslide for about ten years when I went to Rice Krispies. I asked if we could send for one of those special rings. Mom said yes, and I started counting the days. This would be the first, but not the last time I would send in a box top. My situation would not turn out to be the fraud that writer Jean Shepherd experienced with his Ovaltine Decoder. (Read *In God We Trust-All Others Pay Cash*, or see the movie *A Christmas Story*.) But I was to learn one of those small lessons that befall all children.

The ring arrived. It was made of gray plastic and had an opening at the bottom so one size fit all. The "topaz" was a round piece of yellow translucent plastic. Mom said I should wear it on my left hand, where Dad wore his wedding ring. The next day I floated to school, buoyed by the fact that I wore a ring that I was sure would be the envy of every kid who saw it. I got no immediate reaction that morning, but that was okay because we were busy with school matters. Then, at 10:15, came recess. It was a bright and warm sunny morning. I had on a short-sleeved shirt. Nothing would get in the way of the ring that had saved Tom Mix. As we filed out for recess, we exited onto the iron grating of a large fire escape one story above the schoolyard. This would be my first and best chance to flash my prize. I approached the stair-rail and placed my hand on it in a very conspicuous manner, like a young bride-to-be in the office who was just given a one-carat rock by her beloved. No one reacted. Even my deskmate, Paula of the square teeth. NOTHING! I walked home alone that afternoon. Not exactly crushed, but in some vague way an incessant little voice in the back of my head told me that I and my doings were not of great concern to the rest of the world.

Having served up two knockouts to my cowboy dreams, the gods relented and offered an opportunity for a tiny bit of unintentional revenge for Miss Kilroy's cruel edict. When the year had begun, my father had told me that Miss Kilroy had been his teacher at Walsh School when he was a little boy some thirty years earlier. He also cautioned me not to reveal this possibly embarrassing bit of information. I didn't understand why, but Dad said it, so I obeyed it, at least for a while.

By the end of that year I felt I had known Miss Kilroy long enough and well enough to actually get a little personal and confide in her. One day in June, after all my classmates had filed out, I lingered to tell her something I thought would please her. I walked up to her desk and innocently announced, "You were my daddy's teacher when he was a little boy." "Isn't that nice," she replied through clenched teeth, but I thought I saw her nose grow a bit longer. She smiled a strained smile. A strange look came over her face. I got a funny feeling in my stomach.

At dinner that night I told my father about the good news I had given Miss Kilroy that afternoon. He responded, "I thought I told you not to tell her that. Her feelings might be hurt." I didn't know what he meant, but I didn't like the look on his face either.

Chapter 8

We shall not cease from exploration
And the end of all our exploring
Will be to arrive where we started
And know the place for the first time.

T. S. Eliot

Time and freedom. A combination rife with possibilities, promises, and problems. Heady stuff for a youngster. By the time second and third grade rolled around, I certainly had more time and freedom, especially outside our home.

I still did the kid things we all did, by myself as well as with my parents, and enjoyed them. But I started to realize I could make choices of my own, although I think this was not wholly a conscious process. Something in the back of my head compelled me. Instead of being essentially a passive observer, as I was in kindergarten and first grade, I found that I needed greater challenges. Growing up meant getting itchy. I was curious about elements of life within our house like the newspaper and radio, as well as those in the world outside, over the hill, or around the next corner.

I started to become a doer. What I couldn't anticipate was that this would involve much more than pushing a toy bulldozer around a sandbox or feeding apples to the ragman's horse. When we start to take charge of a bigger chunk of our lives, we invariably encounter situations involving risk, responsibility, and, sometimes, moral choice.

My journey into discovery and the assertion of my tiny will in this very large universe began in small ways at home. Some of it evolved from simple attempts to emulate my parents. Once I had learned to read, I could use that ability for something other than the demands of the classroom. I saw my parents read the paper (and books) so I naturally assumed there must be something interesting there. After all, The Waterbury American came every day, and they read it (devoured it, in my father's case) every day. I particularly noticed them reading the comics on Sunday morning. A separate section of the paper, in color no less, would normally catch the attention of any kid, especially at a time when this would be as close as one would come to television or a movie. *Steve Canyon, Terry and the Pirates,* and *Dick Tracy* had enough adventure to light up any kid's imagination. *Prince Valiant,* if for no other reason than the meticulous artistry, provided even more realistic and powerful images. But, with a smidgen of guilt, I must admit that the gunplay of *Dick Tracy* and, for reasons I can't explain, *Kerry Drake* (a private detective), caught my fancy, maybe because both also appeared in our daily paper, so I was able to follow their adventures on a continuous basis.

Tracy's odd, actually bizarre, culprits were riveting. Some have stayed with me for decades. I was particularly fascinated with a strange man appropriately named Fly-face. He was always accompanied by a swarm of flies buzzing about his face, which I imagine played havoc with his romantic life. The situation would be bad enough at, say, dinner with a lovely woman, but I can't imagine how he or she would handle a goodnight kiss. Would she be forced to use the old FLIT gun, that pump-spray insecticide that was in every household?

I think the graphic nature in the artistry of Tracy's creator, Chester Gould, was appealing to little boys caught up in the gun craze of the period, which, today, sadly has moved from the world of make-believe to the real world. Whenever Tracy, or his partner, Sam Ketcham, shot someone, the bullet would pass through and exit the body then be traced like a dancing butterfly before it fell to earth.

Nowhere nearly as violent was *Kerry Drake,* but I got hooked on the storylines, which, though obviously simplistic, worked for a seven-year-old. Again, though, it was the criminal who gave the plotline traction. My favorite was an Edward G. Robinson look-alike dubbed Five Spot. He apparently earned that sobriquet by tipping everyone with five-dollar bills, a considerable amount of money to toss around casually in the late forties and early fifties.

I graduated to comic books soon after but had to mosey down to our local drugstore to do most of my reading. Simply put, I rarely had a dime to buy one. Though I quickly discovered that my mother's metal nail file made it relatively easy to slip coins out of the deposit slot in my piggy bank when I turned it upside down, the guilt of stealing money from something used to save it got to me.

My interest in comic book characters did have a valuable concomitant result. On a page in the back of one comic book I found a simple profile of a girl with the bold print caption: DRAW ME AND WIN A PRIZE. I didn't know it was just a come-on for some type of mail-order art course. I asked my mother if she would draw it. She declined and handed me the pencil. "You try it," she said. I did.

With simple pencil drawings I set out to create larger versions of Bugs Bunny, Sylvester the cat, and Daffy. I always had trouble with Bugs' cheeks, Sylvester's nose, and Daffy's bill. What were initially awkward efforts eventually became recognizable facsimiles. I even tried a little subtlety by shading with the pencil's edge.

I don't know if these crude efforts brought out the perfectionist already in me or simply made me more meticulous, but in my attempts to recreate the characters perfectly, I found that the need for perseverance was absolute. "If you're going to do something, do it right," was one of dad's favorites. Both of my parents were consistently fussy about their work. That instinct kicked in as I got into my twenties, but, regrettably, I didn't apply it in my schoolwork often enough.

One very important part of growing up is finding some kind of hobby or work that is done in solitude, by yourself, for yourself. Such doings provide a lot of self-motivation and can be of great therapeutic value, even for a young kid. I picked up a pencil every now and then for the next several years. I'd get on a drawing jag and do family members and outdoor scenes, but somehow I let it slip away. I wish I hadn't. But I did commend drawing to my own children, and they found as much in it as I did. It's as easy to pass on a good habit as a bad one.

In addition to my occasional drawing binges, I culled two more practical tips from comic books. A *Felix the Cat* comic demonstrated how to make a simple stern paddleboat from a small piece of wood, which would serve as the boat, and two smaller pieces fitted together to form a four-paddle propeller powered by an elastic band. I copied it at my dad's workbench with his guidance and, to my amazement, I had actually made something that worked! From yet another comic I noted how a child character tied one end of a string to his loose tooth and the other to a doorknob. He had his brother slam the door. I had a very loose tooth so my brother, Al, and I carefully followed suit and the tooth fairy visited me that very evening, though I was suspicious about her timing. When I lost my next tooth, my already shaky belief in the fairy completely evaporated when I felt my father's hand slip under my pillow just before he left for work at 5:30 in the morning. This didn't shake my belief in Santa though. I wasn't that foolish.

Funny how tiny fragments of those first outside-of-school reading experiences stuck in my brain. For instance, Bugs Bunny's nemesis, Yosemite Sam, posed a pronunciation problem and a learning moment. When I first saw the word Yosemite, I used phonetics to pronounce it and came up with Yoze-mite. Confused, I asked my mother who informed me of the proper pronunciation as well as what and where Yosemite was. She was amused at my blunder and happy to clarify it. But what really got a laugh occurred when I decided to expand my reading experience and jump to the sports page. I really didn't understand what I was reading about as it turned out. I didn't know enough about the actual workings of sports, even baseball. I knew even less about tennis, but one name kept popping up that I really struggled with. Somewhere in my sports page perusals I came upon the name of tennis star Vic Seixas. I knew last names could be tough to pronounce, but made it even tougher on myself when I unconsciously transposed the letters of his last name to S-e-x-i-a-s. Then, using my phonetic training, I asked my mother who Vic "Sexy-ass" was. A half hour later, when she stopped laughing, she said his name was pronounced "Say-shus." Fine. But what was so funny? Such were the times. I had not yet heard the word "sex" or any of its derivations and it would be several more years before I would.

Chapter 9

. . . This is the music everyone who has ears should hear.

.   Alexander Blok

Whether it be the small Philco on the refrigerator or the Stromberg-Carlson console in the living room, the radio was always on in our house. My mother loved music. She played the piano and, in her younger days, sang professionally with a local trio dubbed The Melody Girls. While dabbling at the kitchen table during my drawing phase, I not only heard the music, I began to listen to it—especially the lyrics. You know. It's, like, we, like, hear Britney sing, but do we, like, listen to what she's, like, trying to, like, tell us? I knew most of the songs were about love, love lost, love found. I had no interest in that, but what did catch my attention was a phrase here and there that evoked an image like "ghost riders in the sky," "mule train," or "see the pyramids along the Nile." The only reason I could "see" the pyramids was because my parents had given me a Viewmaster at Christmas. One of the circular slide discs presented the seven ancient wonders of the world in 3-D.

I didn't have the knowledge of words or the life experiences to appreciate the genius of Cole Porter, the Gershwins, Irving Berlin, or Johnny Mercer. And it would be only a few years before the summer of 1955 would roll around and Bill Haley would ask me to rock around the clock. And I did, for the next couple of decades, at least. Then, slowly, I began to rediscover the music that the old Philco on the fridge had cranked out daily. I saw a Sinatra concert in the early seventies. I bought a couple of his albums, listened, and learned at least one of the reasons why I've always loved studying and teaching poetry. Some of those older tunes contained lyrics worthy of many fine poets, and some of them probably lay dormant in the back of my brain for years.

I should add that all my years of listening to rock did not exclude the modern standards; the great tunes of Bill Haley, Fats Domino, Chuck Berry, and, of course, Elvis moved pop music in a different direction. But there was still room for "Moon River," "Misty," and all the love ballads of Mathis, Engelbert, and Andy Williams, and many more. All these thoughts about the so-called standards can't help but make me wonder what today's kids will have to fall back on when they grow older. Many of them have been raised on hard-edged and essentially tuneless stuff from the git-go. Has the cynicism, vulgarity, and graphic language about sex and violence dulled their aesthetic sensibilities? Would they consider it "lame" to dance to a romantic Tony Bennett, Nat King Cole, or even Paul Anka ("Put Your Head On My Shoulder") ballad?

Unfortunately, being born at the right time probably does, at least in some contexts, make sense. As far as songs that inspire romantic love, idealism, and a gentleness of spirit go, I feel today's kids were born at the wrong time. Of course, no one is really born at the "right" or "wrong" time. Let's just say that some periods are a little less taxing on the head and heart. Nevertheless, when they grow older, I fear today's generation won't have the kind of music that acts as a cultural cushion—something that will soften the daily hassle. Only time will tell and most of us won't be around to see what happens. In a world where the stress quotient increases daily, I hope today's kids will be as lucky as we were. Young geniuses like Harry Connick, Jr., Diana Krall, Wynton Marsalis, Big Bad Voodoo Daddy, and barely-out-of-her-teens prodigy Jane Monheit offer some hope. Will the rest of the young generation find some relaxing moments in the great music of the past? You haven't lived life until you have danced to Johnny Mathis' "A Certain Smile" or have just sat back, closed your eyes, and listened to Sinatra sing "Once Upon a Time."

Chapter 10

. . . "sitting in the catbird seat" means sitting pretty .
James Thurber quoting Red Barber

I turned seven during my last year in the North End, and often found myself in the seat of one kind of vehicle or another, always seeking the thrill of the ride as most young boys always do.

There was no music in my dad's car because there was no radio in his 1940 Plymouth. Since my mother had remained at home that day, the two of us sat together in the front seat and chatted. We had just completed an early Sunday morning ride to New Haven to visit my father's sister Edith, whom I rarely saw. She was not, shall we say, in the family mainstream, but my father felt that a sense of duty came before personal differences. I not only saw Aunt Edith and her husband, Uncle Gene, but for the first and last time, until I visited San Francisco some fifty years later, I saw trolley cars. They looked like street-going trains and trains already had my interest. I also saw white fire engines. How could a fire engine be white? But they were and still are. It's not easy for a kid, and many adults, to get their minds out of one groove. But seeing white fire engines and giving it some thought later helped me to get at least a little inkling that there is often more than one way to do things.

The return trip to Waterbury took only about a half hour on that lazy Sunday morning. We traveled up East Main and had stopped at a red light, about to turn left onto Cherry Street, when my father asked me to slide toward him. I warily sidled over. "How'd you like to help me shift gears?" The actual risk for this kind of maneuver was minimal. Traffic was very light and Dad would, in reality, have complete control of the car. Still, there was an element of naiveté operating here. As I found out when I became father of two boys, young fathers are intent on demonstrating their driving skills for their admiring sons (and I suppose daughters too, today). I think

they also have an unconscious desire to see their kids grow up—
something that really shouldn't be wished for too early. As soon as
a kid could see the hood ornament, he was ready to be introduced to
some of the driving fundamentals. It's no secret that youngsters,
especially little boys, have a predisposition for vehicles of any kind,
and all that that implies. My boys still insist their best Christmases
brought them their Big Wheels and, several years later, their ten-
speeds.

Dad placed my left hand on the shifting lever attached to the
steering column. Placing his hand on mine, he took me through the
three forward speeds, cautioning me not to pull back on the lever as
I went from first to second. Today's youngsters probably wouldn't
realize that such a slight change in the proper shifting mode could
lead to reverse—while the car was moving forward. What would
that do, besides make a grown man cry? Have you heard about those
iron filings your Aunt Emily feeds her hydrangeas to make them
turn blue? Well, that's where they come from. The sound of those
grinding gears, matched by the sound of Dad's grinding teeth, would
bring smiles to a transmission repairman's lips.

We hit third as we climbed Cherry Street past Warden's Dairy
with its trademark giant milk bottle out front. At the next stop he
removed his hand and I actually shifted by myself, relying solely on
his voice commands. I was thrilled to have a part in driving the car.

Many more behind-the-wheel adventures were to follow. Dad
couldn't have known it then, but my "vehicle gene" had been
excited to new levels, and his well-intentioned lesson almost came
back to haunt him and, for a moment, actually placed my cousin Jim
and me at considerable risk. This entire experiment was part of his
trust-building program. But, in the not-so-distant future, I once
recklessly violated that trust. Stay tuned.

On one downtown visit we stopped in fire headquarters next to
city hall on Field Street. My father was, of course, continuing to
make his vicarious adventures mine. A distant relative was on duty
so I got a grand tour, including a slide down the brass pole and, the
very best moment, a chance to climb up to the tiller's seat on the
mammoth hook and ladder. I had to stand just to hold the wheel, but

I envisioned myself racing down Grand Street, steering left when the tractor turned right, communicating with the driver up front through my make-believe microphone. It probably took about a week for my heart to calm down. I continued to make occasional visits to our local firehouse on Walnut Street in the north end, and, after we moved, on Bunker Hill Avenue right across from our school. The firemen always were cordial and answered our questions, which were probably the same with every visit. On a summer's eve we would sometimes sit in one of their captain's chairs and watch the television that sat behind the big pumpers. Even on my visits to see my dad, I still got a little heart-jump when I saw Engine 8 sitting at the ready and immediately recalled names like Seagrave and American-La France.

I had to stand on the low wall next to Junior DeBenedictus' (a.k.a. June Bug) house to reach the seat of his new, maroon Schwinn. He was offering rides and, never having been on a two-wheeler before, I had to give it a try. With an inseam of about six inches at that time, needless to say I couldn't reach the pedals. The good news was that I was facing downhill toward our house on Wood Street. The bad news was that I didn't know how to apply the brakes. No matter.
As soon as I pushed off the wall I knew I was in trouble. As I picked up speed, I was unable to control the bike and plowed right into the privet hedges in front of our house. I arose from the shrubs with nicks and cuts from head to toe. The bike was fine, but, as I recall, all the witnesses gathered beneath our open third floor windows to hear my screams and cries. It seemed as if they knew that when I limped to the top of the stairs, my mother would already be waiting with cotton balls and gauze in one hand and Merthiolate in the other.

I had already assumed a white-knuckled grip even before the next the next memorable ride in my life began. I was about to have my first experience in a roller coaster, in the front seat no less. My dad sat next to me and, as the train of cars slowly climbed to the top of that first precipitous drop, he reassured me that I would enjoy the ride. As usual, he was right.

It was everything you would expect it to be. The stomach-churning, spine-twisting extremes from zero gravity to several G's made me a lifelong lover of these infernal creations. It scared the hell out of me, but I was ready to go again. I think it is actually fear that keeps us going back. In our younger days it's the physical sensations alone that grab us. During the adolescent years it's the need to demonstrate we are not afraid. That's why, especially in boys, there is the mandatory unemotional façade upon entry and exit. The internal screaming during the ride is their secret. During the adult years? Maybe the late, great Grand Prix driver, Mark Donahue, said it best in a fascinating *Sports Illustrated* article I read twenty or thirty years ago. He suggested the race drivers take a car around the corner within a hair's breadth of death's door to prove to themselves that they can face death and walk away from it. But they return to do it again and again, not because they are brave, but because the fear of the Grim Reaper creeps back in and once more they have to face it. But it's the fear that's the controlling factor, not bravery. So, maybe it is that factor, that full realization of our mortality that brings us back to those kinds of rides when we get older.

Curious how strange and seemingly unrelated things connect in our lives. What I could never have realized was that the stress and strain of the coaster was nothing compared to the emotional gymnastics my mother would put us through for the next several years. The day of that first ride at Lake Compounce in Bristol, Connecticut, gave me a glimpse of her darker side. She asked, pleaded really, with my dad not to take me on the coaster. In what was a brief but telling moment, she quietly insisted I not go, but it wasn't just your normal "oh, gosh" fretting. There was genuine fear in her eyes, like that we see in a cat's eyes when it is frightened. Her reaction was out of all proportion to the situation. Here we were on a lovely summer's day in the middle of the music of the merry-go-round, the roar of the coaster, the smell of popcorn, and my mother was in trouble; she was genuinely frightened. The juxtaposition of the two made it like something out of a Hitchcock movie (*Strangers on a Train?*).

The moment passed quickly and I got back to the business of having fun. But that evanescent impression of a behavior I had not seen in my mother before found its way into the back of my brain and curled up there to lie dormant for many years. It was decades, actually, before I was able to recall it and fit it into its proper place so that I could figure out the jigsaw puzzle that would reveal my mother's fragile emotional make-up.

Chapter 11

There is one thing alone   that stands the brunt of life
throughout its course: a quiet conscience.

Euripides

My experiences with seats in different kinds of vehicles ignited new interests, all of which were connected to speed and excitement. But one very different seat might explain an early peek down the road to perdition.

Every month or so, on a Saturday morning, my father and I would walk down Wood Street, take a right on Orange Street, and a left on East Farms. There on the corner was Pat's Barbershop. It had the ambience of an old-time saloon. Except for the light directly overhead, it was dark. The years had taken their toll on the orange-stained tin ceiling that held two fans with large brown paddle blades. There was the dark, hair-covered floor, the wire-backed chairs, and an even darker, more mysterious backroom that reeked a musty odor of tobacco and urine. A spittoon sat in one corner, presumably for the tough old Italians who smoked Perotti cigars which had a distinctly repulsive odor causing them to be better known as "guinea-stinkers." That smell, combined with their oddly crooked shape, gave them the appearance of something not mentioned in polite company.

As the men spoke among themselves, some in Italian, some in English, Pat Travisano, the barber, reached down, grabbed me under the arms and in one sweeping motion swung me into the jump seat that sat atop the regular leather and porcelain barber's chair.

I looked at myself in the mirror and was amused by how my little head seemed to pop out of the white smock, which Pat pinned at the back of my neck. I loved the sound of the electric trimmers. They had an almost hypnotic effect on me. Even today, when the barber chats, I respond, but I'm miles away in a sleepy, restful place.

As he trimmed and snipped, I noticed Pat's arms. These weren't just hairy arms. These were the arms of a creature that swung from the limbs of trees. Many years later, my father related that as young men he and Pat were good friends, and whenever they went to the shore for some sun and surf, dressed in their one-piece, tank top bathing suits then in style, all the guys would remind Pat to take off his "sweater" before he went in the water.

He spun the chair around and continued to fashion my crew cut as he chatted with the men seated against the wall. A strong breeze came through the screen door, and I watched in fascination as the hair on Pat's arms wafted in the wind. And then, as I blew the clippings out of my eyes, I inadvertently looked up, and there she was, high on the wall above my dad's head. She was on a calendar for a local dairy. In one way, I guess that was both oddly appropriate and ironic. She was seated on a couch with nothing more than what looked like a mink stole draped over her shoulders and down her arms. Her honey-blond curls, china blue eyes, ruby red lips, pink cheeks, and other feminine attributes completed a compelling picture. My mouth dropped open. I coughed as hair drifted into my throat. I had never before seen a naked woman. I was, of course, far too young to have any hormonal reaction, but even though I looked away, curiosity drew me back to her. I knew I wore a goofy smile on my face and, for a moment, feared I had been caught peeking. But they kept on chatting local politics and the Yankees, and I kept trying to figure out why there was a picture of a naked lady up there on the wall *with a calendar beneath her* no less. I was confused about this unlikely combination. What I wasn't confused about was that I knew I shouldn't have been looking at her. I inexplicably felt guilty because I had seen something I wasn't supposed to, though I played no part in our meeting. That didn't make sense, but I didn't want to be caught looking. Why? At no time had I ever been given a lecture about nudity. I didn't even hear the word sex until several years later. How had my seven years of life in our society imbued me with a sense of the forbidden when I knew absolutely nothing about gratuitous sex, about what that girl on the calendar was silently mouthing?

There's probably both a good and a bad answer to that question. Songwriter Johnny Mercer asks us to "accentuate the positive," so I will abide by his wish and simply say that I believe, through a kind of social osmosis, we pick up vibes very early in life. If not overdone, if not abused, this can be a good thing. There is no denying that I somehow sensed that this young lady's presence up there on the wall was somehow not completely proper, at least for kids.

And therein lies a fairly obvious lesson. Much of our society seems to have lost a perception of what is inappropriate. Just as a certain societal standard seeped into my subconsciousness then, so now does a kid as easily learn of a world with fewer limitations, less of a sense of what is appropriate. As it turned out, the "show" at Pat's barbershop was only an occasional experience, which came to a close when we moved a few months later.

It would be at least four or five years before I started browsing through the girly magazines (far more innocent than what is on the market today) at Charlie's Drug Store. Even then, when the owner chased us away from the naughty magazines in the corner, that guilt I sensed at the barbershop so many years earlier peeked out from behind the magazine rack, only now he had a new friend with him— shame. I'll leave the reasons for the shame to the sociologists and psychologists. Suffice it to say that members of my generation are all familiar with it.

An afterthought for consideration: I suspect that young parents today would vigorously protest or carefully avoid any barbershop where such a calendar graced the walls. That would be a reasonable reaction. I am equally sure that many of these same parents wouldn't object to dressing their fifth grade daughter like Britney Spears, or letting Junior play with video games that deal solely with blowing characters to pieces.

Why do you suppose that is?

Returning to my earlier remark about traveling the road to perdition. Soon thereafter I actually did take at least a few steps in that direction. I would like to blame the calendar girl, she of the mink stole and nothing else, but she had nothing to do with it. It was my own decision, completely, and even at the tender age of seven I was fully conscious of what I was doing—and that it was wrong.

My mother had taken my brother and me for a stroll up to Walnut Street. There, just across from the firehouse, was a small shop filled with sundries and notions much like a miniature Woolworth store. With my brother in hand, Mom went in search of threads and ribbons or such while I wandered off behind the shelves in search of something more interesting. As I turned the corner into a new aisle, I noticed a collection of toys. Within seconds I spotted it, a Dick Tracy cap gun. The box was no bigger than a deck of cards. It wasn't sealed so I opened it. The silver automatic fit my tiny hand perfectly. Clearly, I thought, this gun was made for me. I had recently become an avid Tracy fan and, like virtually every little boy, I was fascinated with guns. The signs were clear. I was meant to have this gun.

As I slipped the gun back into the small yellow box, I knew I shouldn't even bother to ask my mother if I could have it. In my world and, I suspect, that of most other kids then, I already knew I couldn't have a toy simply because I wanted it. My parents didn't feel compelled to gratify my daily whims. The times for toys were Christmas and my birthday and maybe a token gift as the result of a visit to New York. I learned early on not to even bother asking when I already knew the answer; however, I already had an answer for myself. I slipped the box into my waistband, covered it with my T-shirt, and rejoined Mom and Al at the cash register.

When we arrived home, I told her I was going to play in my sandbox. Surprisingly, she bought it, even though I had abandoned playing there for the last few months. She continued up the stairs, and I returned to the sandbox and feigned interest until she was out of sight.

I knew I was a thief—and worse, a hypocrite. About a month earlier I had left my catcher's mitt atop the hedges in front of our house. When I returned a bit later, it was gone. I frantically and repeatedly searched everywhere, not realizing what had happened. Then, for the first time in my life, came a huge light, a startling revelation. Someone had stolen it! I couldn't believe that I had been a victim of theft. When I reported the crime to my father, I was hit with another blast of reality. He told me it was my job to take care of the glove. He would not replace it. It was three long years before I got another one.

Now I had joined the ranks of the kid who had purloined my glove. But the problem didn't end there. Now I had to bear the burden of guilt—real guilt. I carefully buried the gun in the box. No sooner had I thrown the last scoop of sand on the evidence than my conscience went to work. As soon as I climbed the stairs to our back door, I knew in my own little-kid way that the specter of paranoia had followed me. I was sure my dad would find it. Even if he didn't, how would I explain my brandishing a shiny new gun? Would they notice it was new? Would they see the guilt on my face? Would that Pinocchio thing come into play? Would the gun burst up through the sand and reveal me for the common thief I had become? And what about God? I had not yet had any formal religious training, but my dad had told me about a few of the commandments. Would God zap me with one of those streaking bolts of lightning my dad and I often watched from the back porch? I was in trouble, and nobody but I knew it.

After a restive night, the next morning Jiminy Cricket was right there standing on my shoulder, screaming in my ear, something about letting your conscience be your guide. There was, of course, an obvious and easy way out. That morning I retrieved the gun, carefully brushed all the sand from the box, stuck it in my waistband, went back to the store and placed it where I had found it. And felt good.

Chapter 12

How does it fee
To be on your own
With no direction home
Like a complete unknown
Like a rolling stone?

Bob Dylan

The summer of 1950 would be my last on the streets of the North End. Our home in Bunker Hill, still a work in progress, was only a few miles and a few months away. A couple of early visits had evoked both a sense of promise and confusion. I would be trading an urban environment for what was actually a suburban area that still had a rural flavor. Everywhere there were patches of woods ranging from a half acre to thousands. My imagination was galvanized by the possibilities for adventure and excitement. I decided to hold those wonderings for the quiet moments in bed before I fell asleep. This was, after all, the beginning of summer vacation, and there was plenty of fun and trouble waiting for me on Wood Street.

I had just finished a vigorous morning workout playing "run-down." Anthony and Dan Perrone had a huge play area in front of the several garages in their backyard where my father kept his Plymouth. They had carved two circles about fifty feet apart in the sand, which served as bases. As the youngest, and having virtually no baseball skills, I was chosen to be the runner. They would toss a baseball back and forth while I frantically scrambled between, trying not to be tagged out. That was the first time I discovered I had a little speed. I had never thought about myself as having any special ability. It was their remarks, which gave rise to the thought. They were older than I and had the ball-handling skills to catch me, but they failed more than a few times as I slid safely into "home."

Funny how one little moment like that, one small realization, can make a kid's entire day and give his self-image a little boost.

Bolstered by this new awareness, I raced home for lunch, and bounded up all three flights and in the door ready for the usual fare of soup and a sandwich. Teresa Brewer was cranking out "Music, Music, Music" in her inimitable and somewhat irritating style as Mom started to warn me that the street would be tarred the next day. I was forbidden to get tar on my sneakers and admonished to take them off before entering the house.

Like so many tragic days that were yet to be, I remember that specific day, June 26,1950, only because of the news that came on right after Teresa Brewer's pratings, and because of my mother's reaction to it. I wasn't listening to the news, but my mother was. She had just begun to ladle out the soup when she stopped, put down the spoon, and placed both hands on the edge of the sink. Her head dropped and I was sure I heard a couple of sniffles. I had never heard my mother cry. She quickly gathered herself and quietly cursed. "Another goddamn war," she said to no one in particular. I wasn't sure what cursing was at that point in my life, but I knew it when I heard it. I was upset and concerned. When I asked her what was wrong, she shushed me. What she was listening to were accounts of the North Korean Communists' insurgence into South Korea. The Korean War had actually begun a day earlier, but I guess the moment's news really hit home. Three of my uncles had come home from war just five years earlier. America had just begun to settle into a new era of promise and growth and, though Russia and China were rattling their sabres, I think she, like most Americans, didn't expect a shooting war. Her consternation was real and I felt it, at least for the moment.

Having finished a very quiet lunch, except for a brief explanation of what was happening around the thirty-eighth parallel, I raced out the door and down the stairs, spraying bullets from my imaginary machine gun and proclaiming that we were going to kill all the commies.

But kids have short memories, and the next day my attention turned to the imminent arrival of the street-tarring crew. Time was of the essence. Before the goopy tar crept into the cobblestone gutters, they would be swept clean and a treasure trove of valuable litter would be lost. Amid the countless cigarette butts lay bottle caps and popsicle sticks. The sticks could be used to weave fans or even something to place a hot pan on. These were usually tossed out about a minute after I showed them to my mother. They were dirty, very unsanitary. Disgusting, now that I think about it. Mom was the ultimate clean freak and I suspect, if she had her way, all the street litter would be washed—and ironed—then thrown out. But she allowed me to do the normal little boy things with the dust and dirt of the world, so my play life was not hindered by her obsession.

The bottle caps, however, were critical for one of our street games. Whiffle Ball had not yet been invented, and stick ball games were tough in such a cluttered and crowded environment. We did occasionally get hold of an old tennis ball that had little bounce left in it and played baseball on the street, but even then a good whack would send the ball into someone's hedges or front porch. Our ball chasing became just too bothersome for our neighbors and us.

Before we began our poor man's whiffle ball, we would get hold of a wooden soda crate and roam up and down the street collecting bottle caps from the gutters. A broomstick cut in half made a fine bat. The pitcher, the crate of caps at his feet, stood on one side of the street and winged caps at the batter not more than twenty-five feet away. When kids don't have much, they can become very creative.

It took more than a little skill to hit such a small target, and those that were missed conveniently lay at the batter's feet to be reused. What we never considered was the risk. If someone hit a line drive and the cap were to hit the pitcher in the eye, there could have been very serious consequences. Fortunately, no one ever got hurt. I'm sure our parents never even gave it a thought. Most of our fathers had probably played the same game themselves.

The tarring of the streets was another matter. For a couple of days our play was limited to the sidewalks. In a city of hills it didn't take much imagination to think of ways to add some real excitement and, of course, an equal share of risk to our daily lives. A favorite source of thrills involved roller skates; actually one roller skate and a board about four or five inches wide and a couple of feet long. Maybe an old piece of tongue and groove. Since skates were adjustable, it was easy to shorten one to squeeze the board and hold it in place. Then we simply sat on it, got a firm grip on each end of the board, pulled our knees up to our chests so our feet were clear of the ground, and let gravity do the rest. It was a crude forerunner of today's skateboard.

As we raced down Wood Street's uneven sidewalks, we had about ten seconds to figure out if we should dig in the heels of our sneakers and stop short of the intersection of Orange Street and possible death from a crossing car, or lean hard to the right and try to make the corner to finish the run on a flat and safe surface.

Using the heels of our sneakers to screech to a halt could also bring death by parent. It was a fundamental rule, even in our young lives, that we should get as much mileage as possible out of our footwear. Not wanting to get a lecture about prematurely chewed up sneakers, I opted for the hard turn. As I leaned right, hands firmly gripping the ends of the board only a few inches above the sidewalk, my knuckles met the pavement. I thought about someone taking a rasp to my skin and bone. I thought about blood oozing out of the wounds. I didn't think about the pain—yet. I waited until I got home to Mom, and the Merthiolate.

That last summer on the streets of the North End provided what turned out to be the most frightening moment of my seven years. Three boys, a couple of years older, whose names I cannot recall and, in fact, may never have really known, decided to take a stroll downtown. I do recall that they, like me, were aimlessly roaming around the street late one Saturday afternoon in September. I decided to join them in their walk. The earlier darkness and chilled air added to what was to become a genuine moment of fear and abandonment. Now I laugh. I didn't then.

The walk downtown probably took only fifteen or twenty minutes, even at little-kid speed. Down Wood Street and Vine, into the North Square, down North Elm which spilled out onto East Main

Street, less than a couple of minutes from the green, the bustling hub of Waterbury. I was not a stranger to the heart of the city. On countless occasions my brother and I accompanied my mother on shopping trips as well as her monthly visits to pay our phone, electric, and gas bills. Checking accounts were not part of their lives then, so a quick trip to the Howland Hughes department store, which offered a courtesy window for utility bills, took care of our monthly obligations. Scores of buses pulled up to the south side of the green to drop off and pick up riders. Pigeons foraged for a dropped piece of popcorn. Policemen wearing white gloves helped direct the heavy flow of traffic. On summer days, horses drank deeply from the Carrie Welton Fountain, which was designed specifically for the horse traffic of an earlier day. Handsomely dressed men and women walked quickly from store to store on Bank Street in search of fine clothing and jewelry. Downtown employees grabbed last minute groceries at the Mohican Market, which opened onto the street much like an open-air bazaar in foreign countries. My father's good friend, Mickey Bruno, was a manager and, on one visit, my dad and I met entertainer Victor Borge who lived in nearby Southbury.

All of this is gone now. Sadly, the sterility of shopping malls and strip plazas has replaced it, mostly as a matter of convenience. Downtown life brought people together and created a sense of community, something kids of the last thirty years can no longer experience in most towns. When we speak of an alien culture, people no longer connected, it doesn't take much brain power to see how the disappearance of downtowns has made us strangers to each other and enhanced fears and hostilities that need not be.

So here we were, four street urchins on East Main Street. There were four theaters within a minute's walk. Someone decided we should sneak into the tiny Plaza Theater, which I suspect was part of the original plan. The box office was the kind of glass-enclosed bubble on the sidewalk we now see only in comic strips. We sauntered by the pretty girl in front, did an abrupt about face, ducked down, opened a door and ran like hell into the darkened theater. Like the bad guys being pursued in a Western, we decided to split up.

I found an aisle seat and hunkered down. The movie was about Billy the Kid. This was too perfect. A free movie and a Western to boot. Billy shot a couple of people, as was his wont, and then carved his initials, "W. B." (William Bonnie) into a post. That's all I remember for two reasons: I was too nervous to absorb much more; and the pimply-faced usher suddenly appeared from behind the blinding light in my eyes. "May I see your ticket?" he snickered. Before I could answer, I was getting the bum's rush out the door.

I squinted as I was propelled into the late afternoon sunlight. My chagrin was short-lived when I realized I was alone. All alone. My accomplices were nowhere to be seen, probably having been thrown out earlier.

A touch of panic—how was I going to get home—and a large dollop of fear—my mother's going to kill me—had momentarily clouded my mind. I decided I would start backtracking and if I got lost, I would ask someone where Wood Street was. A couple of hundred feet back up East Main I saw the large yellow brick building that was to become my future home for four years—Crosby High School. That was where I should have made a left onto North Elm and headed back up to the more familiar environs of the North Square. Instead, I kept walking past the school and made a left onto what looked like a major thoroughfare. It was Cherry Street, a broad, busy street. I began the long gradual climb and about halfway up, there before me was the familiar twenty foot high milk bottle of Warden's Dairy. I decided that I was headed in the right direction because my dad bought ice there for summer picnics and we had recently passed the spot where I had had my first driving lesson. The hill grew steeper. I knew I had to be closer to home. As I neared the top of Cherry Street, I thought I had to take a right up an even steeper hill. I was correct, but what I didn't know was that that right, Vine Street, was at the very top of Cherry Street and would have taken me right to my house. Instead, I made a right at the first very steep hill I came upon, Camp Street. A short climb and I came to a cross street, Orange Street.

I looked up at the street sign, read it, and then had one of those moments only a child's logic could summon. I knew the bottom of our street, not more than eight or nine houses away from mine, intersected with Orange Street, but where I was standing offered nothing familiar. I was looking at a large rock outcropping on the other side of the street, and houses on either side, which were unfamiliar to me. I looked again at the sign on the telephone pole. It hadn't changed. And then, not unlike my earlier recounting of how chocolate milk was produced, I came up with the notion that there were two Orange Streets in Waterbury, and I was hopelessly lost. It didn't occur to my provincial mind that streets often ran for great distances and crossed with several other streets. I was caught up in the possibility that I might never be able to get home, forlorn, beyond tears, so, for no particular reason other than utter desperation, I began to walk to my left. And in a matter of no more than two minutes I came upon the intersection of Orange and Wood Street. I recognized where I was and propelled by sheer elation I raced up the street all the way to our back porch. Proud of my small victory, I popped in the back door just as my mother turned off "Goodnight Irene." It was not going to be a good night for Jerry. She was in a mood most foul, something I got used to over the years, and something I never got used to over the years.

She immediately began to complain about my tardiness and though she was right, I could sense it was only a pretext for the real source of her anger. She was dressed for a night out and my dad wasn't home yet. The factories had geared up for the Korean War, so I assume he was working overtime. Whatever the reason, I was the target of her rantings, which, as I was to learn later, were usually more the result of her tendency to over-react to a bothersome situation than to the seriousness of the problem itself. As I ate, I tried to keep my head down—below the line of fire. I certainly wasn't about to talk about my visit to downtown, but even as the verbiage continued to fly, I thought back to the moment I found Orange Street. Though I happened to have walked in the correct direction, my reading that street sign was no lucky guess. I was actually pleased that because I could read, I was able to get home. Though I erroneously concluded that being able to read would prevent my getting lost in the future, I never ventured downtown on a whim again. Actually, the risk was minimal, even though I now know I could have been victimized by some nut, but I had been warned about strangers and their "invitations," and I was made to memorize our phone number which was only five digits in those days.

In light of what I see for youngsters today, the risks I had taken without my parents' knowledge were far less than those allowed kids today, ironically with parental knowledge and approval. When a child spends countless hours of the formative years watching television shows laden with violent and sexual content, or playing video games which are usually even more violent than regular programming, all this as the fatty tissue builds and builds, this is where there is risk—proven risk, risk to both mind and body.

Of course, sitting in front of the TV set in the family room is safe, and having a perfectly safe world for junior has become a major preoccupation for the soccer parent generation which has fallen prey to media hype, especially the "fear du jour" promos used by local television stations and some talk shows.

Playing outside, running, falling, exploring, taking chances is all part of childhood. Fun is in the doing; learning is in the doing; life is in the doing. Not to accept some reasonable risk for a child is to deny that child life.

Given the choice, I'd opt for Orange Street any day.

Chapter 13

In Xanadu did Kubla Khan a stately pleasure dome decree . . .

Samuel Coleridge

Kubla Khan had nothing to do with it, but it was Al and Norma's pleasure dome, especially after twelve years in a three-flight, walk-up cubbyhole in the cramped and aging North End. Our new home, a modest three-bedroom ranch standing on a 50x125 foot plot of greenery in the Bunker Hill section of Waterbury's still largely undeveloped West End, was modest by most standards then, and especially so today here in the Northeast where houses of this size are no longer being built. It's the day of the McMansions with their staggering McMortgages, which can present needs and pressures that can have some very negative effects on the young owners' McLives.

Our new house seemed to offer so much space that at first we experienced a wonderful confusion over how to adjust to our newfound luxury. We had moved in on Thursday evening, October 19, 1950. Why that particular evening I'm not sure, but my mother later told me that she thought the adjustment might be easier if my brother and I spent the next day, Friday, in our new school and then had the weekend to absorb a different environment and not be overwhelmed by the change. That was good thinking. Sometimes her sensibilities and sensitivity were right on target.

That first night my brother and I were put to bed earlier than usual. All of that day's excitement had taken its toll on my new roommate who, for five years, had slept in a small bed in my parents' bedroom, so small was my room in our old digs. We now had twin beds with mattresses and box springs in a large room with a walk-in closet. The beds would, much to my parents' dismay, soon double as excellent trampolines, and the closet would become a wonderful place to hide from my dad when we played hide-and-seek. But I doubt that thoughts about all this potential for fun had impressed my five-year-old brother who was already fast asleep.

It was probably only a few minutes past seven-thirty that evening as I lay silently in my bed, my body levitating about six inches above the mattress. The anticipation of going to a new school the next day, and the even greater promise of exploration and adventure in the surrounding woodlands had keyed my imagination and made sleep impossible.

Suddenly my thoughts were interrupted by a knock at the back door. Strange voices echoed throughout the house where curtains were yet to be hung and the hardwood floors were still waiting to be carpeted. The visitors were our next-door neighbors, Dorothy and Jim Kelsey, who themselves had recently moved to Waterbury from Dearborn, Michigan. Mr. Kelsey was an engineer now working for Anaconda American Brass. His impressive credentials included an Ivy League education and a war experience of near heroic proportions. He was a young naval officer serving in the South Pacific on the aircraft carrier *Hornet*, from which Colonel Jimmy Doolittle launched the first bombing raids over Tokyo in April of 1942. During late October of that same year, in a fierce clash with Japanese naval forces, the *Hornet* suffered several hits, which proved fatal. Jim Kelsey was running across the flight deck as one torpedo exploded, buckling the wooden deck. He suffered a broken leg, eventually ended up in shark-infested waters as the great ship began to go down, helped rescue others, and managed to survive until he was picked up. I was impressed. So was the government. A few years later he had just made the rank of Commander in the reserves when he received a presidential invitation to the launching of the *USS Nautilus*, the first nuclear-driven submarine. His wife, Dorothy, a Canadian by birth, was the epitome of true class. She was kind, considerate, gentle, and soft-spoken. Not a bad start in a new neighborhood.

This thoughtful welcoming committee of two brought a cake to officially greet their new neighbors. Though there had been hellos as the house was under construction, this was a time to sit and chat and set the tone for a relationship that would remain warm and friendly for many years to come.   I could hear the laughter bouncing off the walls and smell the coffee brewing. I knew I was in a good place. What I didn't know at that tender age was that Bunker Hill was more a state of mind than a place and was as close to Xanadu as I would ever get.

I awoke the next morning to Patti Page singing "The Tennessee Waltz." Mom was preparing breakfast to the accompaniment of her newfound friend, Hartford radio personality Bob Steele. He was the most popular morning man in Southern New England.   Steele provided just the right mix of news, weather, and chatter, blended with a five-part children's story each week. He also offered some terribly corny jokes, a daily lesson in word pronunciation, the expected offerings of pop music, some oldies from the twenties and thirties, and some tunes that defy conventional description. Those who have heard such gems as "Buffaloes On My Lawn" know whereof I speak.

I mention all this because this radio icon helped to ensure that we didn't begin the day as targets of my mother's often unpredictable moodiness. Simply, Bob Steele made her laugh. When she laughed, my brother and I breathed a little easier; went off to school in a more positive frame of mind.

Another staple of my morning routine was Rice Krispies served in a bowl with a portrait of Hopalong Cassidy astride Topper at the bottom. For some inexplicable reason that bowl stayed with me until I went to college. In spite of the pleasure of Bob Steele's and Hoppy's company, in a small way breakfast became a love-hate situation. The orange juice was fine and I loved my cereal, especially with bananas, but somewhere in this country, in a dark, web-infested laboratory known only to a few, some sadistic medieval scientific types decided that cod liver oil (say it slowly, then think about it for a moment) would prevent children from contracting any disease known to man, give them better bowel movements, and make them smarter. They were right about the last part, only it was a delayed reaction. Many years after watching my mother take out that quart bottle of Squibb's Cod Liver Oil and pour it into my waiting tablespoon, I became smarter, or at least smart enough to figure out that I and millions of other kids were part of a brilliant marketing scheme that made Squibb's profits climb—and my heart sink. I would plunge the loaded spoonful in my mouth, suppress my gag reflex, swallow, and immediately chase the horrible aftertaste with a six-ounce glass of orange juice. I remain convinced that all of us who experienced this early morning ritual developed not only a toughness uncommon in youngsters, but also fostered an unspoken promise that someday, somehow, we would get even with our parents for this unspeakable cruelty committed under the pretense of giving us better health.

To be fair, I have to admit that their efforts actually should be lauded. I shudder when I think of what many parents feed their children today. I have seen kids walking to school with cans of Pepsi in their hands at eight o'clock in the morning after a sugar-laden breakfast treat, if, in fact, they had any breakfast at all.

I am not so naïve to think that my bowl of cereal was a model of nutritional excellence, but it was half-filled with milk, which is far better for a growing child than soda. Though my generation did have a limited choice of cereals, that choice was only minimally the result of television advertising, which admittedly had begun early on to push products that would appeal to youngsters' desire for sweet foods. I should also note that there was some variety to our breakfasts. My mother served eggs, pancakes, or hot cereal, like Cream o' Wheat, because she had time to prepare them. Time is not easy to come by in most of today's households, especially in the morning. There can't be a true breakfast moment when there is no parent there, when both are off to work before their children leave for school. Though that situation is so often a matter of necessity, it is no less unfortunate that so many kids have to fend for themselves. Even more regrettable are those parents who simply don't care, who let their children eat whatever they choose, regardless of how it will affect their performance at school, their dietary habits, indeed, the rest of their lives.

There is an even sadder aspect to this scenario. Beyond the problems a belly full of sugar can bring is the loss of an important part of a younger child's life—an oasis of relatively peaceful sanity before the hectic school day begins. Even the ritual of just fifteen minutes spent at the breakfast table with at least one parent can come to mean that home is more than just where one lives. These kinds of moments give a child's life some stability and at least a small sense of security, the value of which goes beyond words.

As I listened to my cereal snap, crackle, and pop, I grew a bit more apprehensive about going into a new class at a new school, not knowing how well I would fit into a different environment. Though it had lasted only six weeks, my third grade class at Walsh School back in the North End had been a completely enjoyable experience. My teacher, Miss Dwyer, was gentle and effective. The learning material, a developmental reader a step up from Dick and Jane, contained interesting and more factual information, while it further developed our vocabulary and phonetic skills. We also continued to review our number facts so crucial to simple adding and subtracting. Reviewing and repeated drilling not only reassured those who readily understood it, but also gave those who were a little slower time to catch up. Today, the material is taught, a task is given, and the class moves on, and young parents are impressed, and administrators and school board members take bows—and so many of the kids forget what they learned shortly after the test, if they learned it at all.

The illogic of what we sometimes do in the classroom virtually screams out at us. Astronauts train for years; Tiger Woods hits hundreds of golf balls each day; and Michael Jordan has taken hundreds of thousands of practice shots (and publicly complained that people seem to think his success is simply the result of talent and not the product of countless hours of practice). And yet we continue to delude ourselves into thinking that because a child can demonstrate a recently learned skill, or regurgitate information only a short time after being exposed to it, that he has mastered the subject.

This is neither the first nor the last time I shall sing my song about the value of repetition and drills. In looking back at my own education and having seen what I saw in my last few teaching years in the classroom (even at the college level), it is clear to me that all the talk we hear about the lack of basic skills in today's students is not just talk. Ask Michael Jordan.

*****

In addition to the new learning material, the first month (and my last) of third grade back in Walsh School was highlighted by a Parents' Night. Miss Dwyer gave a demonstration class while parents stood at the back of the room. A box supper followed. Then benches were set up in the hallway. When an unfamiliar machine was rolled in, I knew I was in for a treat even though I had never before seen a film projector. I was engrossed by the few movies I had already seen in theaters, but the thought of being able to see one right there in school was cause for more than a little excitement. Aside from later viewings of Cold War propaganda films which offered Nike missiles blowing B-29 drones (surrogate Russian bombers) out of the sky, or a roomful of dummies near an atomic test site being tossed about like, well, a roomful of dummies in the aftermath of a nuclear shock wave, this half hour film, which was less an adventure and more a travelogue about a young Indian brave's discoveries in the wilderness, was the only audio-visual experience I was to have in all of my grammar school years.

What I do remember about this brief color film, with only a voice-over narration, is that it completely engaged my emotions. I still remember what I felt, in spite of my dim memories about the story. What brought back all those feelings about that film I saw on Parents' Night more than fifty years ago was a similar experience I had with my own boys in the late seventies. As part of a Cub Scout gathering which involved parents, the Cubs were to be treated to a short film, originally produced in 1966, entitled *Paddle to the Sea*. The live-action film was based on a wonderful award-winning book of the same title, published in 1941. In many ways, by virtue of its unassuming simplicity, I saw it as being uncannily similar to the film I saw that evening in 1950.

It is the story of a young Indian in his early teens living in Canada, north of Lake Superior, presumably in the late 1930s. Involved in the fur-trapping industry, he sensed his life would probably always be confined to that area. He longed for an adventure his situation would almost certainly never allow. Out of a single piece of wood he carved a twelve-inch long canoe with a tiny Indian figure at the helm. He then meticulously poured lead into the keel for ballast so it would always right itself and provided a tiny rudder for stability.

As spring approached, he placed his model in the snowbound country high above the river valleys. The melting snows carried his surrogate traveler, whom he named Paddle-to-the-Sea, into a small stream, which would be the beginning of a four-year journey down rivers, through the Great Lakes, over Niagara Falls, up the St.Lawrence Seaway to the Atlantic. As one might expect, Paddle encountered a variety of perils in his quest, including river rapids, forest fires, huge cargo ships, and aquatic animals. All threatened his journey, but none was any more serious than just washing up on shore.   Fortunately, the youngster had the foresight to carve a request on the bottom of the canoe: "Please put me back in the water; I am Paddle-to-the-Sea." In what amounted to a nice message for youngsters, all who found it cooperated: one even repaired damage to the battered canoe, and Paddle completed his journey to the sea.

This Oscar-winning film offered virtually no special effects, only a voice-over narration, and the frozen visage of a carved wooden Indian. I remember that simple thirty-minute film now, almost thirty years later, not only for its content, but also for how effectively it engaged my nine-and-seven-year-old boys as well as me. As surely as this film began as a vicarious adventure for the young creator of Paddle, it became my boys' adventure as well as mine. The child in me was still there—and still is. We were not merely witnesses; we became participants. We sat beside Paddle in that tiny canoe. Our imaginations invested his expressionless face with fear, determination, and joy. His perils became ours, his success our triumph. *We* made it to the sea.

Though my boys and I viewed it from different perspectives, I was busy watching them as well as the film. I now realize, some thirty years after that 1978 viewing, and more than fifty years after that film experience at Walsh School, that we would not be mistaken in assuming that there are not many of what we might consider simple films out there for kids today. A constant assault of whiz, bang, crash, as well as graphic and overwrought special effects can, indeed have, dulled their imaginations. To be sure, careful and limited use of special effects, for instance in such children's movies as *Babe* and *Stuart Little*, can wonderfully enhance story and character. But an over-indulgence in those elements can easily distract a youngster from the story itself, if, in fact, there is a story at all. Too much of the spectacular gimmicks in most of today's children's films (and in too many of adults' as well) begin to act like an opiate. Our kids become addicted and need a "fix" in every film and become focused only on titillation which only drives out the sense of wonderment and joy in a young child.

The imagination is like a muscle. Exercise it and it develops and grows strong; deprive it, and it becomes weak and withers. This can become more than a temporary problem. Once that power of imagination is lost in a young child, as I often observed in the classroom, it is difficult, if not impossible, to revive in adolescence.

Back at Walsh School the film slapped against the projector as it ended and the lights were turned on. Parents said their good-byes, gathered up their youngsters, and headed for the door. I looked back for the last time. *Ave et vale*, Walsh Grammar School.

*****

Breakfast eaten, hands and face scrubbed, teeth brushed and, lest I forget, gastro-intestinal tract properly lubricated, our trio of newcomers set out for the short walk to Bunker Hill Grammar School. My brother Al wasn't in a stroller this time. He was headed for kindergarten.

Instead of turning left and walking down the street, my mother inexplicably walked to the right. About three houses later, there on the left, we found ourselves looking down a fairly steep path of asphalt about one hundred and fifty feet long. At the end of that was a flight of twelve stairs, then three much shorter walks and three more flights of stairs, the last of which deposited us at the level bottom portion of Circuit Avenue where it intersected in a broad "Y" with Valentine Street. Circuit Avenue, our street, was shaped like a horseshoe. The bend was a steep, uphill curve, without sidewalks, and heavily wooded on both sides—not safe for a youngster to walk. The four hundred feet of tarred path and stairs we had just negotiated allowed for about a forty-foot vertical drop between the top and bottom of our street. Known to all simply as "The Stairs," this walkway provided safety for all of us in the Mount Vernon section of Bunker Hill, as well as a moment of dangerous high adventure that was still a few years off.

A quick hundred yards down Valentine, a glance to the right and there, on Bunker Hill Avenue, stood my new school. Red brick, huge double-hung wooden windows, a cupola with a clock on top, two stories in front growing to three in the rear section as the school was built on a downgrade. A huge elm on either side set off the modest portico in front.

We walked up the five or six steps to the double doors in front, and down the hallway past classrooms abuzz with activity as school was about to start—and found we were late, for my class that is. What my mom didn't know was that the third grades were on double session. Though the baby boom is supposed to have begun in 1945, it began in 1942 in Bunker Hill, in a manner of speaking. There were simply too many of us to conduct regular all-day sessions in the third grade. Some attended the morning session from eight o'clock to noon. The afternoon classes went from twelve-thirty to four-thirty. The problem was resolved the next year, but for that first year I would attend the morning session. Since my class was already well underway, I would be prevented from making a quiet, unheralded entrance. New kids, at least at the outset, usually prefer anonymity.

Our first stop was at the principal's office. As his secretary worked on the registration papers, our principal, Ralph Carrington, made his mandatory welcoming appearance. I would guess he was in his late fifties. He was the kind of fellow you would expect to see in a counting house in nineteenth century England, very much a Dickensian character. He was a small, round-shouldered man with a short neck, hooked nose, and weak smile. As I later observed, he brooked no nonsense from unruly kids and had the annoying but probably justified habit of poking a miscreant at the base of his neck with the first two fingers of his hand. It certainly got their attention. Today's parents would probably have him drawn and quartered for such behavior. I later discovered that the students called him "Gyp," or was it "Jip?" I never learned why.

What I did learn decades later was that he was a pretty good guy who knew his stuff and was respected by the teachers with whom he worked. The city apparently felt the same way when, many years later, it built another school further up Bunker Hill Avenue and named it after him.

Looking back, what I probably saw in him was his "game face," something I would see in some of my teaching colleagues many years later. As I walked the hallways of the school where I taught, I heard and saw some teachers in their classrooms who bore no resemblance to the same ones with whom I ate lunch in the teachers' room. I'm sure this kind of behavior is not limited to schoolrooms. Boardrooms are probably no different. What I do find curious is the belief that wearing a mask is necessary, at least in the view of many teachers, most of whom are probably not even aware they are doing so. A teacher can be friendly and still be a fair disciplinarian. As a student, I always felt more comfortable and far more motivated when I didn't have to sit there and fear the grim look in front of me. Wearing a mask is a dangerous thing. It not only keeps the students off-balance, but, as George Orwell points out in his most wonderful short story, "Shooting an Elephant," if someone in a leadership position wears a mask "his face grows to fit it." Kids like a real person, and that day, as luck would have it, I was about to meet one.

The principal's knock on Miss Connor's door was answered by an attractive, smiling woman who was, as I later discovered, in her late thirties. Her prematurely silver pixie cut and sterling rimmed glasses complemented her sweet smile and bright eyes. Her energy and enthusiasm immediately made me feel comfortable. Introductions made, Mom's predictable last words whispered, "Behave yourself," Miss Connor's introduction to the class offered, I was led to the last seat in the last row and given a book. The class was already in the middle of an oral reading exercise.

She pointed out the page and paragraph and returned to her desk. I read along with the student who was reading aloud and tried to size up the class at the same time. Would these kids be any different? The boy next to me wore a white shirt and tie and looked smart. As I was wondering why he was dressed so well, he was called upon to read. I was right. He was smart, and I was a little intimidated. The next reader was a cute little thing in the very first seat. She took complete control of the moment. Her facility with words and reading was apparent. She completely captured my attention, so much so that I barely heard my name called, partly because I was not used to being addressed as Jeremy. I had not been in my new class for five minutes, and I immediately realized this was my first let's-see-what-the-new-kid-has-for-brains test. I read for what seemed like a disproportionately long time. When I finally heard Miss Connor say "thank-you, Jeremy," I looked up to see her reaction. Teachers always are anxious to see if their newest addition to the class is going to be a problem. She smiled; I beamed.

No sooner had I settled into my new class than I could hear the distant tooting as it grew closer. Sure enough, a couple of days later the Tonsil Train pulled up to our house. I think it was part of the same bandwagon mentality that gave us that inimitable taste treat, cod liver oil. Medical science combined with young mothers' desire to raise perfect kids is a force not to be denied. Somehow, in the late forties and early fifties, it was revealed that tonsil removal (and while you're in there Doc, don't forget the adenoids) would make us healthier and happier little tykes. That train hasn't been back for decades, so I guess the jury is out on the beneficial effects of a tonsillectomy. Nevertheless, several decades ago it gave many of us our first look at the green tile (I had imagined it would be white) of the surgery rooms at Waterbury Hospital.

My brother and I were bedded in the same room along with two other victims. Our pediatric surgeon, Dr. Merriman, stopped by that afternoon to tell us what we could expect the next morning. He was tall, distinguished, and gentle. He eased the little anxiety I had. I was also relieved to see he spoke in a normal fashion. My pediatrician, Dr. Brown, had the curious habit of sticking the tip of his tongue out of the side of his mouth whenever he wasn't speaking. It became a minor but amusing, actually hilarious, issue when we went for check-ups. My little brother and I would set each other off to giggling even before we got to his office. And my mother threatened to kill us if we laughed in front of the doctor, who, by the way, was popular and very competent, according to my uncle Guy Sandulli, a fellow physician who practiced a few doorways away. I looked forward to those visits not only because we invariably came out of his office cackling, but also because my mother would get caught up in the moment and start laughing along with us. She looked so pretty when she laughed. It was one of those few moments we had with her in our younger years when there was no tension—just an easy moment of lightheartedness.

Meanwhile, back in surgery, the nurse held what looked like a tea strainer a few inches above my nose and asked me to count backward from ten. She poured a few drops of ether into a cloth in the strainer. I started to count; the table began to spin faster than the merry-go-round at Lake Quassapaug. I don't think I made it to five.

When I awoke, there in the bed next to mine lay my brother doing a remarkably good impression of Vesuvius, which devolved into more of an Old Faithful, and finally calmed to an occasional burp. I think I did a little better only because I was a little older. As our heads and stomachs cleared, the rescue squad arrived with ice cream and Jell-O topped with whipped cream, exactly as predicted by neighbor Joan Kelsey who had already undergone the procedure.

A few days later I returned to school, now with my unseen red badge of courage. Miss Connor informed the class that I had had my tonsils removed. I was embarrassed. She was probably trying to allay the fears of those yet to undergo the procedure. I confess that memory of that moment may not be totally accurate, but I did expect to form a bond with those classmates who had undergone the knife, and hoped to provide counsel and comfort to those about to. I think we all do after a trip to the hospital. In a small way, however, I felt special. A nice little ego trip. Then I discovered something I often rediscovered throughout my life. Nobody cared. In spite of present day classroom bulletin board proclamations that each child is special, the fact is that we may be special to our families but not to everyone else. A piece of humble pie every now and then is good for a kid's psychological diet.

*****

The rest of my third grade academic year went smoothly, as it usually did in classrooms that were sheltered from the distractions that can come from the world outside. This, of course, is the only proper learning environment. The school atmosphere promoted learning by focusing our attention and providing a high comfort level. This is probably true at most levels of schooling, but nowhere is it more necessary than in the early grades. Rarely did matters of the outside world, such as politics or social upheaval, come into the classroom. Except once.

One day in late spring a cold hard reality of growing concern to the adult world quite unexpectedly stuck its ugly nose in the door of Miss Connor's class. It was the only bump in a year that otherwise was to play out perfectly. I don't remember if it was a question from a student or if Miss Connor had initiated the subject. Considering what was happening on the international scene and America's involvement in it, I suppose almost anything could have triggered that moment when the tension, fear, and urgency of the Cold War first blew into my life.

So much came to bear on the American psyche so quickly that, in retrospect, it was no wonder Miss Connor had reacted as she did. After all, Ethel and Julius Rosenberg had just been sentenced to death, the Korean War had begun just a few months earlier, the Berlin Airlift was only two years past, the Russians had tested their A-Bomb in 1949, Mao had taken over China that same year, and two very dangerous men, one theirs, the other ours, had taken to saying and doing dangerous things. In February of 1950, Senator Joe McCarthy sharpened his tongue and started "finding" communists within our own government. The numbers he uncovered depended upon the mood he was in on any given day. The other guy was Joe Stalin. We didn't have a television yet, but those grainy A.P. photos in the newspaper, which my mother took time to point out, were enough to tell me that that snarling smile belonged to one scary bastard.

With all this pressing on America's collective consciousness, it was inevitable that a classroom moment would somehow come around to THE BOMB. Miss Connor began to explain that it was incredibly powerful and that it required only a very little amount of "stuff" to make a terrible explosion. At the same time some of us, especially the boys, with their limited exposure to caps and small fireworks, knew that it takes a lot of "stuff" to make a big explosion; the more stuff the bigger the bang. Miss Connor went on to explain that the bomb was made with atomic material (she probably said uranium) and that atoms were very small. Some of us began to doubt the accuracy and credibility of her explanation. The smirks and smothered snickers were apparent to all of us and to her as well. As a last ditch effort to make clear this atom business, she said, "You don't understand. An atom is smaller than . . . than . . . a pea."

We burst into laughter. No, we didn't think she was trying to be humorous. We were laughing at her and what we perceived as the ridiculousness of her statement. "No, no. You don't understand. It's true." More laughter. Then, without warning, that pretty, perky face drooped and from behind those silver-rimmed glasses came tears, big tears, tears of fear, confusion, consternation, and most of all at that moment, tears of frustration. Why couldn't we see that she was truthful, that she was warning us that our young lives could be in jeopardy? She heard our ignorance in our laughter; saw our innocence in our faces.

Did she really want us to know then what would soon enough become a reality in our lives? Probably not. It's not fair to weigh down a youngster's spirit with the madness of the adult world. I'm sure she knew that. She simply did a very human thing. She wanted us to know of the danger so we could protect ourselves; so she, as an adult, could protect us. It's the way we would like life to be.

Miss Connor's tears immediately brought a halt to the giggles; even caused a few of us to cry. She cleared her throat, said she was sorry, then began to smile. Nervous laughter broke out on both sides of Miss Connor's desk. We moved on to other matters of the moment, our emotional balance and our protected, sheltered classroom restored.

Our family purchased our first television set that same year in October of 1951, and soon I saw some of the A-Bomb tests from Yucca Flats, Nevada. Even a young mind could sense the horrific power. By the summer of 1952, on warm evenings as I lay beneath my open bedroom window, I often heard the unmistakable drone of a four-engine plane going into Brainard Field up in Hartford. Sometimes I wondered if it was one of their planes, not one of ours. Lying there in the warm, quiet darkness, in my mind's eye I could see the bomb bay doors in the belly of the plane slowly opening. I would grit my teeth and hold my breath until the hum of the engines was swallowed by other sounds of a summer night. Only then, feeling safe, would I breathe a deep sigh of relief, knowing that this was not *the one*.

It was then that I began to understand what dear, sweet, tearful Miss Connor was talking about.

Chapter 14

. . . when like a roe
I bounded o'er the mountains, by the sides
Of the deep rivers, and the lonely streams,
Wherever nature led.

William Wordsworth

At the top of his final exam in Zoology 110, Al Avitabile, one of the finest professors I ever had at the University of Connecticut, quoted the nineteenth century French naturalist Jean Louis Agassiz: "Study nature, not books." As luck would have it, I started thinking along those lines years earlier, only a few days after reaching Bunker Hill.

Just as the Kelseys, our next-door neighbors were the first to greet my parents, their older daughter, Joan, two years my senior, was my first greeter. A knock on the backdoor on the first Saturday in our new home mercifully interrupted the Ames Brothers' mind-numbing ditty "Rag Mop." Joan had come with an offer to tour the immediate neighborhood. As it turned out, my blond, freckle-faced docent, fiercely bright and very articulate, was the perfect guide to the wonders offered by my new environment.

We took a right out of the driveway as Joan set a brisk pace and initiated a running conversation about my new neighbors as she pointed out their houses, noted their names and whether or not they had children.

In the space of little more than one hundred yards we had passed a couple of streets on the right, both, I noted, ideal for sledding, "The Stairs" on the left, and then, two houses later, the pavement disappeared and abruptly narrowed to a sandy path in a heavy tract of woods I would now guess to be about ten acres. The size of the trees and the darkness of the forest floor indicated most of the land had been undisturbed for a long time, maybe forever.

Joan walked me to the end of the path, which brought us out at the quiet corner of Adelaide and Woodruff Streets. She pointed to the left and there, just a hundred feet away, was Circuit Avenue. This was the other end of our horseshoe shaped street, which, of course, I had never before seen. She said she wanted to show me this short cut in case I got lost. A smart move. I hadn't forgotten getting lost on Orange Street.

On our way back up the path, fifty feet off to our left, I saw the remains of foundation footings for a home that apparently became no more than someone's unfulfilled dream. We walked along the top of what was once a floor plan and now only moldy and crumbling stones that clearly had been mortared together many years before. A tiny rill slowly moved through what might have become someone's living room. Joan scared up a leopard frog, which should have already found its way into the mud for a long winter's sleep.

As she was explaining this to me, she began to laugh. It was my gaping mouth and wide-eyed stare. She had no idea that I had never before seen a frog like this. What she didn't, couldn't, understand was that for my first eight years, with the exception of a few excursions into the countryside, I lived surrounded by nothing but asphalt and maybe three trees. Strangely, all these years later, that parcel of land remains exactly as it was on that day with Joan. In a part of town that has little land left on which to build, it still stands as the sole reminder of my earliest connections with the wonders of nature.

On our return from the end of the street, Joan didn't stop at our homes. She continued to walk down the beginning of the steep curve, past a few more neighbors for whom she also supplied the names and other vital statistics. We approached yet another, larger patch of woods where some sizable boulders separated the pavement from a quick drop down to a small pond. We carefully moved down the moss-covered ground of a hill that was heavily treed. There were few lower limbs, but there was a heavy canopy of leaves above. The hundred feet of green incline didn't get much sun, even in the summer. Because of the sharp angle of the hill and the slick moss, which ran all the way to the pond's edge, we gingerly took the last few steps toward the water.

I'm not sure if "pond" is the right word. This tiny body of water, then with a dark bottom covered with decaying leaves, couldn't have been more than fifty feet wide and probably measured a bit more than a hundred feet long and, as later exploration revealed, was no more than three feet deep. The spring-fed water was quiet and cold, absent of any signs of life. I asked if anything lived in it. Joan knelt down and turned over a rock by the water's edge. And there, as if on cue, out scooted a salamander. This two-inch long creature wasn't pink or red as were my later findings. Black, and covered with bright yellow polka dots, it looked like a tiny dinosaur in a clown's suit. I was awed by its beauty and its resemblance to its much larger and horrific ancestors, which I had seen at both the Peabody Museum in New Haven and the Museum of Natural History in New York.

I was equally impressed that Joan knew about such things. Sometimes kids can teach each other more effectively, or at least spark more curiosity, without any of the encumbrances of the traditional teacher-student relationship. Her sheer enjoyment of what nature had to offer in a real-life setting touched me. There was not going to be a test; I didn't have to learn it. She simply wanted to share her sense of wonder.

It worked. The pond and all it had to offer was to become a gateway to a world that will always have a special place in that list of things to which I give the highest priorities in life. I'm sure Disney World is fun, but parents can so easily take their youngsters to those places that can give them insights to a world and wonders they might not otherwise know exist. Admittedly, however, there are fewer and fewer of such Edens thanks to our ever-expanding land developments.

We walked to our right to the pond's outlet and carefully stepped along the top of a crumbling stone and mortar dam, apparently built decades earlier. The water ever-so-slowly trickled over the top of the dam and into a steep downgrade covered with skunk cabbage, a low broad-leafed plant with stalks that looked something like celery. She whacked a couple of the plants with a dead tree limb, and within seconds the foul odor told me how skunk cabbage got its name.

The other side of the pond was clear of any heavy growth and the ground gently slid into the shallow water. It was here, on our ensuing visits in the late spring and early summer, that I learned how prolific this small body of water was. During the warm months this side of the pond caught the full power of the sun. In the quiet, grassy shallows in what was like some kind of primordial soup, life flourished. Joan pointed out clumps of frogs' eggs, which were little more than small black spots in globs of gel. A few weeks later she introduced me to tadpoles, which she noted were commonly called polliwogs. Some of the larger ones were sprouting legs and then it dawned on me that these ungainly looking creatures, tiny bowling balls with tails, were on their way to becoming frogs. One look and I could see all the stages of development in one shot. This was interesting stuff, and Joan correctly guessed it would work its magic on me.

I was clearly frightened by the dragonflies, also called sewing needles. My guide was nice enough to point out that they could sew up my ears if I got too close. I may have been a product of urban life, but she couldn't fool me. Within two years I figured out that they were harmless. And, like most of nature's creatures, they were more frightened of us than we of them, with good reason.

I loved the way the water spiders skated across the smooth surface, and how an occasional muskrat in the weeds at the far end of the pond would, at the sound of our voices, execute a crash dive looking much like a gray, hairy submarine. There were also water snakes slithering through the weeds, rushes, and cattails, with thick black and brown patterned bodies that made them look genuinely dangerous. Rumor had it that these were cottonmouths and were deadly. This bit of local knowledge, however, was about seven hundred miles north of the truth. Painted turtles, as well as an occasional weasel, also found a comfortable home here. A few years later one young trapper swore that he caught a mink.

I found all of these critters remarkable, each in its own way. But what I didn't realize was that so many wonderful kinds of life could be collected and could thrive in such a tiny place only slightly removed from human traffic. It now seems more like the stuff dreams and nightmares are made of, except science indicates otherwise.

The land behind the sunny side of the pond, all of it soggy wetland populated by thin, seemingly malnourished trees, rolled gently downhill for about two-hundred yards to Bunker Hill Avenue. This strip of land continued along the avenue and also ran behind our house until it climbed to thousands of acres of meadows, fens, and woods. The pond was the only body of water of its kind in the area. The spring that fed it and the sun that warmed this fragile eco-system created a perfect niche in which things could happen that otherwise might not have. When the aquifer that fed the spring dropped, the water became stagnant until the next rain. But this condition allowed the water to become even warmer for a short while, and the inhabitants apparently found it even more desirable. And so did we—Ricky Lorton, Phil Beach, and I. This became the primary gathering spot for the three of us, until later, when the lure of baseball (then religion for young boys) and simply growing older turned our attention in other directions.

As for me, Joan Kelsey, probably to this day, doesn't know that her enthusiastic and informed introduction gave me not only an abiding and active interest in nature and conservation, but it also gave me the one spot I consider a sacred part of my childhood. It was the focus of some of my best moments and some of my most introspective a year or two later.

I believe all kids should have a spot that is their own, a place which, in the words of Wordsworth, when "the world is too much with us," they can escape to and find a gentle and nourishing solitude. A place where they can sit, look, and not have their minds cluttered by so much of the silly stuff we adults engage in. A place where our minds and natural surroundings become one. A place where we can find a peace that goes beyond words.

Chapter 15

To me, fair friend, you never can be old,
For as you were when first your eye I ey'd,
Such seems your beauty stil

William Shakespeare

A new neighborhood and new school naturally brought new kids, some of whom became friends for life. The first two boys I met, Ricky Lorton and Phil Beach, remained my best friends for many years. Phil and I still maintain contact and see each other on a regular basis, mostly on the golf course. Ricky and I remained close friends until life took us in different directions. Though I rarely see him, when I do, my heart knows we have a special bond that will be there as long as we live.

I met both during one of my four daily trips up and down "The Stairs" to and from school. Rick lived right at the bottom of the stairs, and Phil lived atop Wayland Avenue, which began just around the corner from my house. During our first few years together, we pretty much did what a lot of little boys did then—we played outdoors, something that seems to be lost on many of today's youngsters. Except under extreme conditions, we spent virtually all of our playtime outside, letting each season dictate different activities.

Our earliest adventures involved playing "guns." That's what we called it—not playing cowboys, not playing soldiers, just playing guns. If we wore pistols, we were cowboys; if we brought our toy rifles, we were soldiers. These were no-frills games. Though the pistols were always cap guns, we still supplied our own sound effects. Somehow it seemed more realistic. Two of us would seek out the other one; or one of us would search for the other two. There was a small hilly patch of woods behind Rick's house, which provided ideal conditions for ambushing each other.

Plans would be made on the way home from school. We would meet and play until we grew tired of it, or it became too dark (though dusk offered the best opportunities to sneak up on the bad guy), or until we had to go home for dinner. It was a game with a lot of running around and few rules. The goal was simply to have fun.

Why did our play involve guns? Because little boys are fascinated with them, whether they are water guns, cork guns, cap guns, ray guns, B-B guns, or just a thumb and forefinger. It's a fact of life in America and, without examining all the reasons, psychological and otherwise, that's just the way it was, and still is.

For my generation, the burgeoning legend of the cowboy as part of America's heritage grew larger than life through the power of radio, television, and the movies. This began in the late forties and carried right into the late fifties when, believe it or not, for a short while, there were more than twenty Westerns on television every week. Cowboy gear—boots and spurs, Stetson hats, fringed cowboy shirts and cowgirl skirts, and, of course, the mandatory set of pistols—were popular gifts for us young buckaroos.

The impact of World War II and Korea also wasn't lost on us. Whether it was a photo in *Life* magazine or one on the piano of Dad in uniform, G.I. Joe or Combat Kelly in the comics, or even memorabilia Uncle Harry brought home from overseas, the images and weapons were never far away.

Our parents had a much more liberal attitude about these kinds of toys because they were just that—toys. They were not seen as symbols of a society that had become violent and dangerous, of a country where guns are used by young people to kill other young people in the streets and, incredibly, even in the schools.

Most of us went through our gun phase and then moved on to other interests. As adults some of us went on to hunting, but the need for high-tech weapons of every possible description, which were solely designed only to kill humans, was not there. There were no video games to give us the opportunity to simulate blasting humans, or humanoid creatures, to kingdom come. There were no movies whose horrific graphics both initiated and even justified any dark thoughts or needs that might be sitting in the reptilian portion of our brains. Honestly, I don't think many of us harbored such thoughts, and, in any event, a civilized society should know better than to nurture them. What really makes all of today's killing games so utterly reprehensible is that not only are they created solely for profit, but that parents buy them for their children, not recognizing that they are destroying the innocence that kids need in order to be kids.

Meanwhile, back at the ranch, Ricky, Phil, and I did have to abide by one rule before we played guns, or anything else, especially when school was in session. We had to change into our play clothes. Why am I reminded of such a seemingly minor consideration? Because kids today wouldn't have to change clothing. Therein lies a regrettable social statement, not only about how we view school but, sadly, about how we seem to have abandoned a sense of propriety, and the need to understand how important a touch of formality, and I don't mean tuxedoes, can be for children and the adults whose responsibility it is to guide them.

In spite of the endless lip-service pumped into the media about how special school is, about how concerned we are about the education of our children, so much of what we allow in schools runs contrary to that ideal. As a teacher, and as a student, I always believed that school was a special place. That's not to say that I always liked it. But always beneath the vicissitudes of the school experience lay the belief that this was my work, my job, just as my mom and dad had theirs. I knew that these doings were serious and important business. Part of that came from home; part of it came from the school itself. There were clearly expectations.

Of course I didn't articulate such thoughts as a youngster, but what I did have, what all of my classmates had, was an ability to pick up vibrations. I believe all kids are equipped with internal antennae that detect and define signals from the moment they are born. One such signal about school's importance was that we dress in a manner befitting the occasion. I had three sets of clothing: Sunday-go-to-mass clothing, school clothing, and play clothing. Each mode of dress sent a clear message about the nature of what I was doing.

We have become a casual, more laid-back society over the last four decades. I even recall the interest the media had in noting that President Kennedy did not wear a hat to his inauguration. President Eisenhower had worn a homburg. Maybe that was the beginning for the boomers and maybe that was as it should be. Too many of our sartorial choices were far too restrictive and ridiculous, if not downright uncomfortable. But, like so many of America's choices over the last fifty years, we have now gone over the top in the other direction. In many quarters we have moved from a casual society to just plain sloppiness, or should that be "slobbiness." Kids get the message. The way they are allowed to dress for school today tells them school is not special, not a place where they are required to take their appearance and behavior up a notch. For all too many there is no distinction between play and school.

That is not a good thing. It can easily be corrected, if we are indeed sincere in our purported concern about kids' behavior and attitude in and about school. Appropriate dress tends to evoke appropriate behavior. Even young cowboys knew that.

What Ricky, Phil, and I didn't know at that tender age was that our pursuits would tend to be the same throughout our childhood. As luck would have it, we always enjoyed doing the same things. I don't know if that was because we drove each other's interests, or because we were somehow cut from the same cloth before we met. At any rate, we would come to share countless adventures, all of which bound us as if we were born of the same mother.

Chapter 16

Forgive, O Lord, my little joke on Thee
And I'll forgive Thy great big one on me.

Robert Frost

Though born Roman Catholic, from all I can gather my parents didn't become regular churchgoers until we moved to our new home. I was placed in catechism (later changed to Confraternity of Christian Doctrine) classes shortly thereafter. Formal religious instructions began in second grade so I was a year behind. I was placed with the second graders of Blessed Sacrament Parish and would receive First Communion with them. The next year I returned to my own age group.

Before these years I had had no formal religious training. We occasionally walked to mass at St. Stanislaus, a nearby largely Polish parish. Why we didn't walk just a few steps farther to St. Lucy's, the Italian stronghold in the North End, I am not sure. The Pastor, Father Scoglio, was known citywide as a tough, old, autocratic type, not a rarity in the Catholic Church in those days. Though my father was unquestionably demanding of my brother and me, in some clergy members I think he saw that tendency as a very different application of power. He was training us to be good kids and, therefore, good adults. What he didn't like, however, was an adult who pushed around other adults, especially when that person was supposed to be God's representative on earth. Simply put, he felt those who represented Jesus should emulate Him.

Some of the old-time priests and nuns abused their power, but frightened parishioners were not about to speak up. My father was not one to shrink from confrontations when he felt them necessary, but with church matters he felt it wiser to avoid them. Except once.

I was about to be baptized at St. Thomas' Church about a month after my birth. In making arrangements, the priest asked under what name I would be baptized. My father said, "Jeremy." My mother and father didn't know what was coming next, but I suspect the priest did. He informed them that my name would not be acceptable. The problem was that the spelling of the name Jeremy was found in King James' (Protestant) version of the New Testament. The Catholic version, the Douay-Rheims Bible, called for Jeremiah. The priest's reasoning did not sit well with Norma and Al. As it was related to me, after a bit of a go-around, it was clear neither side was going to budge. They agreed that my middle name, Joseph, would be my baptismal name.

The priest was satisfied, but this small event left a bitter taste in my dad's mouth. My mother never seemed to carry that same anger, possibly because Joseph was her father's name. I was named after my paternal grandfather, probably because we shared the same birth date, October 2. Both grandfathers had died shortly before I was born, so I suppose my parents' choice of names carried more than a little emotional impact.

What rankled my dad, as he explained years later, was how the Church could assume that God would be upset if I were baptized Jeremy instead of Jeremiah. He wondered why so much importance was given to such a piddling issue. His beliefs were centered on the larger picture: that religion should help people behave well toward each other. He hung his philosophical hat on the tenet that we should always try "to do the right thing."

Apparently he was not alone in his thinking about archaic and largely senseless small stuff. Just two decades after my visit to the baptismal font, Pope John XXIII called the Vatican Council II with the intent of examining the Catholic Church's position in the modern world. More enlightened thinking brought us, among other changes, the mass said in the vernacular instead of Latin, though, I must admit, I miss hearing what poet Robert Browning called "the blessed mutter of the Mass." In 1966, when I married my wife Irene, a Lutheran, we were allowed to have the first nuptial mass for a mixed marriage at my parish, Blessed Sacrament. I think the whole ecumenical movement helped to make the church more Christ-like, and that was a good thing.

Unfortunately, a kinder, gentler approach was not yet in place when my religious instruction began. My father had taught me the "Hail Mary" and "Our Father" when I was about five, but in the little red house next to Bunker Hill School, I was to learn a lot more, some of it, I'm sure, not very pleasing to the Lord.

Except for the second and third graders who met on Saturday mornings, all other Catholic students in school were released at 2:30 (the rest remained in school) to attend catechism classes in a small, unoccupied, red Cape Cod style house adjacent to the school. The classes continued through eighth grade and were taught by three or four nuns from the church, which was about a mile away. It was a convenient arrangement and, if there were legal questions about the church-state relationship, they were apparently never raised. This was not surprising in a town with fifteen very active Catholic parishes.

I would be less than honest if I didn't note that I found my classes to be neither enjoyable nor productive. What we learned was solely the result of a regurgitative process that made little or no connection between God and our humanity. We memorized and gave back what we read in our Baltimore Catechism, and in many cases were far too young to sense its meaning. We learned about mortal (serious) and venial (less serious) sins. We were told that the Catholic Church was the one true church, a thought that didn't do much to encourage tolerance, especially in the mind of an impressionable child. We learned that we should not marry someone outside of the faith, except under grave circumstances. (I guess I blew that one.) There was more but not much. The same things were rehashed year after year. The only thing that changed was that we had to buy a new Baltimore Catechism every year, which would be a different color. Still, we were innocent kids and most of us took it fairly seriously, although as we moved up a grade each year, it was clear that some of us began to take the whole experience less so.

After the fifth grade, the year we were confirmed, the boys and girls were separated. There was at least one sweet and gentle nun, but she always taught the girls. My six years of instruction were limited to the tutelage of just two nuns. Sister Immaculate

Conception was quite elderly and was clearly prone to some "super-senior" moments. She usually called me Germany. I did not correct her. When my classmates chuckled, they were laughing at both of us, but I thought the joke on me was okay. My father had always lectured about having respect for elders and I did, especially for this non-threatening, gentle old soul. In this case, however, my feelings went beyond that. I felt sorry for her; in fact, she might have been the first person for whom I had a genuine sense of compassion. She had spent her life doing God's work and still had to deal with us, not always a sympathetic group. I even remember the sway and click of the giant set of rosary beads she wore around her waist as she limped around the room. I had instinctively decided she was not going to get any trouble from me.

Such were not my feelings for our other instructor, Mother Superior. She was somewhere in her fifties and made most Marine drill instructors look like a bunch of pansies. I laugh now, but not then. And that was part of the problem with the religious instruction approach in those days, at least in the Catholic Church. A reliance on the threat, the or-else attitude, hurt, if not obliterated, the attempt to bring us closer to Jesus and his teachings. I suppose she taught us as she had been taught, but that kind of approach just didn't work with us.

Mother Superior had two prominent buckteeth and a high nasal voice. These, combined with a slender appearance, gave her an uncanny resemblance to Bugs Bunny in nun's habit. Unfortunately, she had none of the humor of her Looney Tunes look-alike. And that led to a memorable moment, though not one I'm proud of.

One early spring afternoon in sixth grade, when we returned to school after lunch, Bill Scavone, one of my classmates, had what we agreed was a brilliant revelation. Bill's remarks caught our attention and generated immediate and keen interest for two reasons. Though he was the same age as us, he had gone through the transition from boyhood to young manhood much earlier than we. (It was rumored that he started shaving in third grade.) Consequently, we assumed that he had more courage than the rest of us. The other reason we followed his lead was simply because it presented an opportunity for revenge. And the target would be Mother Superior.

Bill proposed that we all switch jackets before catechism. Then, at some point in the lesson, he would stand and point at one of the other boys and yell, "Hey, you've got my jacket." Others would then follow suit. All agreed.

The moment came. Bill stood, pointed at Pete Petrarca and cried out in mock anger. Pete pointed at Bill Schofield and so it went, a chain reaction among twenty boys that sounded like a string of firecrackers going off. I sneaked a look at Mother Superior. As a cacophonous chorus of morons followed their script, she was baffled—for about five seconds. As we put on our own jackets and began to calm down, she didn't miss the smirks and smothered giggles. What a coup! we thought, but she was no fool. As the dust settled, a thin smile began to spread across those gleaming white choppers. She didn't have to ask, "What's up Doc?" She knew. And she would soon even the score.

About a half hour later the lesson for the day was finished without further incident. Mother Superior had not made one allusion to our moment of planned madness. I think all of us were naive enough to believe that we had won a small victory. As we got up to leave the class, Mother Superior "suggested" we kneel, say a few prayers, and ask the Lord's forgiveness for our disruptive behavior. The "few prayers" turned out to be not one, but two rosaries. Forty-five minutes and 118 prayers later the hard oak floor had taken its toll on our tender knees. She smiled and thanked us as we limped off toward home.

She won the battle, but she never won our hearts and minds. In fact, our behavior during other religious exercises was very good. During the Children's Mass in the basement of the church at 8:30 on Sunday mornings, as many as 250 to 300 kids would sit, kneel (on wooden kneelers), stand, and actually remain quiet during a sermon which was usually given by a visiting priest from one of the Eastern bloc countries or Southeast Asia. And who usually had an accent too thick to be cut with a ginsu knife.

The well-behaved moments were not attributed to our catechism classes. The credit for that goes to our parents and the society we lived in, both of which asked for courteous demeanor and self-restraint from kids and adults alike, especially when they were involved in serious doings. Religion is by its very nature serious business and plays an important part in the lives of many, and children certainly should learn the doctrines, dogma, and rituals of their parents' religion. But their sense of right and wrong must first be ingrained by the words and actions of their parents. In the home is where the seeds of morality are sown. And even though formal religion can help take some of us through life, I believe finding God is an intensely personal experience, a road we must ultimately travel by ourselves.

And when I find Bill Scavone, I have to remember to thank him for his inspired idea so many years ago.

Chapter 17

No warmth, no cheerfulness, no healthful ease
No comfortable feel in any member—
No shade, no shine, no butterflies, no bees,
No fruits, no flowers, no leaves, no birds,
November!

Thomas Hood

The fall of 1951 brought painful revelations about my parents that made life confusing and very difficult for several years. Though I am clearly both befuddled and angry about how our children are raised today, I would be less than honest if I suggested that my upbringing was ideal. My older cousins, who babysat for me in my pre-school years, told me that my mother's interaction with me had already begun to take on negative overtones when I was still very young.

My first clear memory of the direction my life would take within my household began on a bleak Saturday morning in November of 1951. I know it was a Saturday morning because I had just finished listening to a children's program on a local radio station. It was called *Big John and Sparky* and opened with the theme song "Teddy Bears' Picnic." My mother loved to sing along with the opening lines of this charming ditty:

"If you go down in the woods today
You're sure of a big surprise.
If you go down in the woods today
You'd better go in disguise . .

Phil Beach arrived with his cap gun just as the show ended. I grabbed my plastic shotgun and we were off in search of a good spot in which to play. But when I returned from having gone down in the woods that day, my mother would be singing an entirely different tune.

We found a place in a patch of woods at the end of Elmhurst Avenue, a short dead-end just behind my house. The biting November cold was more than we bargained for. My hands were freezing, and the ground was already too hard to take a running death dive. We decided to cut through the backyard of the last house on Elmhurst to get to my yard.

As we walked into the driveway, on our immediate left we noticed two tiny reflecting pools not more than six by three feet. One was surrounded by small rocks and the other was more like a square metal tub sunk in the ground. They must have been part of what in the summer months was a lovely flower garden and may have even contained goldfish. On that day, however, they were already covered by a wafer-thin coat of ice. The water was muddied and, as we soon discovered, no more than six inches deep. With my plastic shotgun and a dead limb that Phil found, we began to poke through the ice. This was not an act of vandalism. We were merely curious.

As we turned to leave, a screech came from behind us. We spun around to find an elderly woman closing fast and yelling at us. Phil, sensing this was going to mean trouble, wisely turned and fled. Unfortunately, I hadn't yet developed a strong survival instinct. I had reasoned that I had done nothing wrong and therefore had nothing to fear. That kind of naiveté has dogged me most of my life.

I stood my ground and tried to explain that we meant no harm. All the while my gun rested in the crook of my arm. "Don't point that gun at me!" she shrieked. Then I knew I was dealing with a curmudgeonly old woman. I had started to walk toward my house when she demanded to know where I lived. I pointed and she took me by the hand.

When we got to my backdoor, my mother greeted us. My captor introduced herself as Mrs. Curry and, with a voice that sounded like fingernails being drawn across a blackboard, she launched into a tirade. My mother apologized for my actions. Mrs. Curry went home and we went inside.

I was grounded for a week, although a stern warning to stay out of other people's yards would have sufficed. I didn't protest because I knew it wouldn't do any good, because it was my least favorite month for outdoor activities, and because I believed that parents were perfect, and thus were correct in whatever they did.

Slowly over the years, I began to hear and see a recurring pattern in my mother's words and actions. I began to realize that the punishment for the Mrs. Curry incident was just the first of many that reflected my mother's emotional reaction to her own tortured logic, or should I say, illogic. She created myths both small and large, let them simmer until they reached a boiling point, and then visited her rage on me, her closest and easiest target.

I can accept that she was embarrassed when Mrs. Curry brought me to our backdoor. Parents don't like to have their children embarrass them. She drove her point home: Don't shame the family. I think this is a perfectly acceptable tenet in the rulebook a kid should live by. And even if my punishment were disproportionate, parents have to be allowed to make a mistake now and then.

As time went by, however, my mother would rail on about "these damn Bunker Hillites." As a child I thought she was saying Bunker Hill "ikes." Then it dawned on me that she was talking about an imagined corps of elite that stood in judgment of interlopers like us, Italians from the North End. It was her own paranoia ,which was fed by an utter disregard for the facts. Of the sixteen homes one could see from our front walk, it was true that four belonged to white collar professionals: a salesman, an engineer, a banker, and the C.E.O. of a successful, medium-sized manufacturing company. What she failed to see were the homes of four mailmen, a teacher, a cop, a fireman, a lineman for the power company, an upholsterer, a car salesman, a truck mechanic, and a low level municipal functionary. She saw herself tied to the lower levels of a caste system that was nothing more than a figment of her own imagination.

These false perceptions were only part of a larger problem. My mother was what would be termed in those days as "nervous." She was not a happy person, was never content. It wasn't that she wanted more; it was more like she didn't know what she wanted. Her moodiness and mercurial temperament were demons she couldn't get a handle on and, for several years, they became my nemeses as well as hers.

On more occasions than I care to remember, for no reason apparent to me then, she would overreact and threaten ("I'm going to send you to reform school") for nothing more than coming home from school a few minutes late for lunch. I had already been primed for trouble by my dad, who always talked about the importance of honesty (e.g., my Pinocchio episode) and not being afraid to stand up when I had done no wrong. Adding to the problem was her cordial, warm, and loving behavior with all of the extended family as well as her friends and mine. I was further frustrated and felt I must be doing something wrong since I was the only object of her wrath. My mother's cutting and salty tongue finally started to evoke less than civil responses from me. She saw this as nothing more than sass, which only exacerbated the situation. Inevitably would come the words I dreaded most, "Wait until your father comes home." Those very words were the title of a short-lived animated television comedy around twenty-five years ago. It's the kind of phrase many of my generation chuckle about when they reminisce. I shudder.

When my father came up the stairs from the basement after a fun-filled day working with fire bricks and mortar in a cramped furnace, before he could utter a word of greeting, my mother would hit him between the eyes with, "Do you know what your son did today?" (For some reason my younger brother never figured into the equation).

Even though what I did was usually not the issue, the fact was that he did not like family disruption. I was perceived as the cause. I would then get a beating. Even when there was no physical abuse, there was often criticism, some of it bizarre. For instance, whenever I fell ill, it was my fault. This pattern was repeated more times than I care to remember until one night in eighth grade. He was about to let me have it yet one more time, when, though I was a skinny little kid about a half foot shorter than he was, I screwed up every ounce of courage I had, grabbed both of his wrists and said, "No more." I think he had tears in his eyes. I know I did. And that was the last time he hit me.

I think my father had known for some time that I was not the cause of the familial chaos. He found himself caught between the proverbial rock and a hard place and subconsciously reasoned it would be easier to deal with me than my mother. They both realized that this craziness had to stop. For whatever reasons, life in the house mellowed a bit and, throughout that very difficult period, there were even some tranquil and good moments. But the uneasiness lingered. The emotional wounds were slow to heal and the scars remain.

All of that might have been easier to bear if my parents at least occasionally had given me a hug, a kiss, or a kind word. Truth be told, I have virtually no memory of ever having been hugged or kissed by either of my parents. There were critical remarks and neutral remarks, but never praise and encouragement. Good grades or bad, making the Little League team, singing in the park department's barbershop quartet, winning medals in the city-wide track meets for youngsters: none of these brought praise or criticism. I truly believe they assumed that I knew they were proud, that I could divine their feelings without hearing a word of encouragement. In fact, the only words of praise I ever heard from them came through my wife when I was twenty-four years old. As I stepped up to the stage to receive my master's degree, my mother whispered to her, "We're very proud of Jerry, but we would never tell him."

A superb housewife, she kept an immaculate home, was an excellent cook, a very talented baker, had the skills of a seamstress, and could mend almost any playground wound. My father worked very hard, put in a lot of overtime, took side jobs on the weekends, and could repair anything in the house. I think they assumed that my brother and I saw their ferocious efforts as acts of love, and at least part of them may well have been. But they forgot that we were children. A little attention to what we were doing would have provided much of the motivation that we otherwise had to provide for ourselves.

My mother was always too busy to take a moment just to have a conversation with me. And my dad was so busy saving money for tomorrow that he often forgot to use some of it to enjoy today. We never took a family vacation, just the four of us, together— a mistake I didn't make with my own family. It doesn't have to be fancy or expensive. Just one week a year at a lake or by the ocean can strengthen family ties and help eliminate future friction.

I offer these painful memories not because I wish to visit my childhood misfortunes upon others. Those are now part of the past and all has been forgiven; and I have found fair recompense in a wonderful family of my own. But I do want to make clear that the joy and exuberance in much of this story is not the result of an *Ozzie and Harriet* home life.

What I have also found, in retrospect, is that I came through that rough period of my life reasonably intact. My life outside of our immediate household compensated for much of what was lacking within. What saddens me is that I'm not sure many kids today can find the same sense of love, security, and encouragement outside of the home because of the changes our society has seen over the last several decades. Some of those changes are not a matter of right or wrong; they are just a natural part of an evolving society. Simply put, many of us who grew up just before or with the boomers were luckier because, if there were discord in the home, there was a more stable society to fall back upon outside the home, like the extended family.

Most of my parents' generation did not raise large families, but came from large families. My father was one of three children, but my mother was one of eight (thirteen, had not five died at birth). Altogether I had seventeen aunts and uncles and seventeen first cousins. I was met by one or all with open expressions of love. Family meetings invariably began with my face being covered in lipstick and my cheeks temporarily disfigured from hard and lengthy pinches. Family gatherings, especially on my mother's side, had a festive, celebratory flavor. Whether at Christmas, Easter, or Thanksgiving, at Uncle Lou's cottage on Long Meadow Lake in Bethlehem, or at Aunt Lena's cottage on the shore at Bay View in Milford, all were centered around the joy of being together. Everyone treated everyone else with warmth, dignity, and a healthy dose of teasing. No matter what the situation was at home, here I was unconditionally accepted and loved. I was somebody, and I belonged.

My Aunt Marie, who had been partially crippled by polio as an infant and was childless, made her nieces and nephews her surrogate children. She took me to countless movies. *Showboat's*, "Old Man River" and glittering color, *Song of the South's* "Zip-a-dee-do-dah" and the use of animation with live figures, and, believe it or not, "With a Song in My Heart,"from the film of the same name about singer Jane Froman's near tragic plane crash, are still emblazoned in my memory. I even got to see a vaudeville show at the Loew's Palace with Frankie Carl's orchestra, a juggler, and, yes, a pigeon act. All of these stay with me.

My Aunt Mercedes, the only single member of the family, and my Aunt Louise constantly encouraged me about going to college. Whenever we met, there were always questions about school. Aunt Merce gave me books and a subscription to *Children's Digest* and, later, at fourteen, *Time* magazine. My mother's oldest brother, Guy, had graduated from Harvard and Tufts Medical School. His three sons, somewhat older than I, had attended some of the country's best schools. For whatever reason, his wife, Louise, took it upon herself to push me toward higher education. She always talked with me about it and even sent me college catalogues.

The large extended family has gone the way of the two-dollar bleacher seats at Fenway Park. Future generations will not likely have the benefit of the support, love, and dignity that this type of family can provide. If they weren't there for me, I'm not sure how well I would have held up during those difficult times. The one thing I am sure of is that I miss them and the good times we had together.

Just as my extended family provided a cushion to soften some of my life's harder edges, society, from the end of the war until the assassination of President Kennedy and all the madness that followed, provided somewhat of a comfort level for all of us. As children we were pretty much oblivious to major political, economic, and social issues, but we still could sense the calmer tenor of the times. There was a regularity and steadiness our tender psyches could latch onto.

Whether fathers were white-collar employees at Hartford's insurance companies, or blue-collar workers at Waterbury's brass factories, those jobs were secure for life. Today, that security is gone. Corporate takeovers, foreign job markets, and American spending habits, to name just a few, have taken stability out of the workplace and brought a certain amount of consternation, fear, and sometimes chaos to American households.

Even though America was rapidly moving from an urban to suburban society in the forties, fifties, and sixties, once people moved in across the street, more often than not, they were there to stay for the rest of their lives. Add that to neighborhood schools and stable two-parent families and it's not hard to see how kids had a greater sense of security. Today's uncertain job market and a highly mobile society, combined with the demise of neighborhood schools and a fifty percent divorce rate, make it very difficult, if not impossible, for youngsters to retain the sense of well-being that we enjoyed. And if we did have moments of uncertainty, anger, or rage, we didn't have an entertainment media all too willing to feed and exploit those emotions.

To be sure, many of these changes are here to stay. But what is most troubling is that we, all of us, seem oblivious or indifferent to the devastating effects these same changes are having on a whole generation of youngsters. I so often see my friends and relatives throw up their hands and suggest we are helpless and hapless. I think neither is true. Our seemingly self-destructive society absolutely can deal with at least some of the barriers to a stronger family unit. For example, religious consideration aside, I have always been troubled that we feel the need to have our stores open seven days a week. I realize that our mothers had much more free time than today's working mothers, but, while today's moms are shopping on Sundays, both they and the millions that must staff those stores are losing time with their families and friends—time that, once lost, can never be regained. In fact, among the leading industrialized countries of the world, Americans take the least vacation time. There's much to think about there.

Surely a country with our intelligence and resources can still figure out a way to work within the confines of those inevitable changes to give our children at least some measure of the stability we had a generation ago, that same sense of hope and stability that I saw slowly drain from my students' faces over the last few decades.

Chapter 18

In educating the young, we use pleasure and pain as rudders to steer their course.

Aristotle

Kids are surprisingly resilient and can bounce back from less than pleasant circumstances—if they are busy. My run-in with the curmudgeonly Mrs. Curry and all the familial aggravation that ensued were tolerable because I didn't have time to dwell on them. Fourth grade brought more than a few diversions, including our first television and a very different kind of teacher.

It was the fall of 1951 and Nat King Cole was singing "Too Young," *I Love Lucy* was about to debut on CBS television, and *From Here to Eternity* was a best seller. Senator Joe McCarthy, Joseph Stalin, and Chairman Mao were all trying to scare the hell out of us; Ed Sullivan, Marilyn Monroe, and Mickey Mantle were on their way to becoming part of Americana, and President Truman had fired General MacArthur. And on a September morning of that same year, I met my fourth grade teacher, Miss Grinnell.

As we entered the classroom, she directed us to find our names on a piece of oak tag on top of the desk to which we were assigned for the year. We remained seated and quiet until the bell rang, then we were asked to stand for the Pledge of Allegiance, "God Bless America," and the Lord's Prayer. The pledge and song went smoothly; the prayer, however, presented a problem. Miss Grinnell was the first and only Protestant teacher I would ever have in grammar school. As she began to recite the Lord's Prayer, we dutifully followed along—until the end. The Catholic version ends with ". . . and deliver us from evil. Amen." The Protestant adds, "For Thine is the kingdom and the power and the glory forever and ever. Amen." The question I was rolling over in my mind was, do I risk God's wrath (having been properly indoctrinated) for uttering the Protestant version, or do I risk offending Miss Grinnell's religious sensibilities. I made my decision, and I hoped God was busy with something else at that moment. I was, after all, in alien territory. My religious training barely acknowledged other religions, and I knew I was in the presence of a charismatic and imposing figure. That General's cap with the scrambled eggs on the brim that President Truman knocked off MacArthur's head would have sat well atop Miss Grinnell's gray curlies.

Don't get me wrong. It wasn't that she was an imperious type; rather it was her supremely confident attitude blended with her absolute passion for teaching that gained my immediate and full attention. My instincts were correct. She pushed hard and got results, not because we feared her, but because she seemed to have an unshakable belief that we could learn more if we were pressured in the right way. She would accept no less than our best efforts. She was a veritable Vince Lombardi of the classroom; the kind of teacher we have all had: the one who, against all logic, we would swear taught us everything we ever learned.

We continued to work on the skills we learned in the primary grades, but now we began to apply our math and reading abilities to specific subject areas and different reading materials. We were introduced to word problems in math, early events in American history, the geography of Europe and the Western Hemisphere, some fairly sophisticated poetry, book reports, regular visits to the school library, and, a staple of school systems throughout America, *My Weekly Reader*.

Though I am sure there were some kinds of curriculum guides, I suspect Miss Grinnell went beyond those parameters. What we did in our class was not always the same as what Miss O'Connor's class did across the hall, though her class was composed of kids with the same range of abilities as ours.

I suppose Miss Grinnell's independence is best exemplified in how she taught us to subtract: she did not employ the conventional method of "borrowing." I knew her way was different because my parents and friends were confused by the method I used. In fact, it was so different that I used it to demonstrate to my English classes that there is often more than one way to solve a problem, be it a writing problem or any other. With the exception of one student, over 3500 at both the high school and college level were surprised to see there was another method of subtraction. As I would try to make a point about writing, the other half of my brain was trying to determine why Miss Grinnell deviated from the norm, though many math teachers have told me they liked her method. One thing is for sure—she did. And, by God, that was what she was going to teach.

While others were learning the capitals of the states and those of South American countries, she threw in the capitals of Europe. We read poems like Joyce Kilmer's "Trees." I was astonished to learn that Joyce was a man. I liked the clever metaphor "a nest of robins in her hair." She also read Whitman's "O Captain! My Captain" and explained the connection to President Lincoln's assassination. This was fairly sophisticated stuff for youngsters who had never been exposed to much more than the simple rhymes of "Twinkle, Twinkle, Little Star."

The ultimate challenge came when we copied Sir Walter Scott's wonderful "My Native Land" from the blackboard (mimeographs were not yet part of our school experience). We had to memorize it and look up the meaning of words like "pelf," "wretch," and "concentred." We also were baffled by the phrase "foreign strand." This was not easy material for fourth graders to understand, but with the memories of some of those song phrases ("See the pyramids along the Nile") already planted in my mind, her clear but simple explanations about images, and our own rudimentary "research," made these lines stick forever.

"My Native Land" was of course about pride in one's country. I have no doubts this particular poem was part of her reaction to the chest-thumping of the Soviets whose propaganda ministers were telling an angered and outraged America that they had invented everything from the light bulb to toilet paper. She was fighting back. Her unflagging patriotism was always just below the surface and popped up in some unusual ways. We sang songs like "The British Grenadiers," which worked well for me because, as a veteran of countless battles in Ricky Lorton's backyard, I had hurled many grenades (rotten apples, actually) at the enemy.

She gave us plenty to chew on but never overwhelmed us with homework. Twenty minutes to half an hour at most. She also did something others did not. She would, with sufficient warning, re-quiz us on material covered perhaps two months past. I learned to match capitals, such as Bucharest or Budapest, with their corresponding countries through this teaching method, and because her belief in the importance of this kind of general knowledge colored all of her lessons.

The term "cultural literacy" didn't become part of the American vernacular until years later, but that's what it was. I think she believed that there was a body of knowledge and terms that we needed to know to become good students and good citizens. It worked. My parents always watched the news after dinner, as did I, but not because I had a burning interest in the news itself. Though it was my interest in that new piece of technology in the living room, our television, that captured my attention, still, when Edward R. Murrow or Robert McCormick talked about London, Paris, or Moscow, I may not have known what they were talking about, but I did know *where* they were talking about.

In addition to furthering our fundamental skills and introducing us to cultural literacy, Miss Grinnell pushed hard for just plain old book reading. This would be the first year we would make bi-weekly visits to our school library. She often recommended books, as did my friends and the librarian. My friend Phil Beach suggested *Ben and Me*, a story narrated by a mouse who lived with Benjamin Franklin, and *Mr. Revere and I*, a story about Paul Revere narrated by his horse. Both were engaging and genuinely charming stories set against a backdrop of colonial America, a wonderful and clever combination that enhanced our reading skills and provided a lesson in American history. Anything by Dr. Seuss was also a must read. His cover illustrations alone compelled any curious kid to see what was inside.

Speaking of what was inside, I should note that before *Playboy* there was *National Geographic*. I don't know why or how, but it didn't take us long to discover the bare-chested ladies of Africa. It also didn't take the librarian long to hear our smothered snickers and giggles and direct us to something a little more enlightening. Newbery Medal winners, the annual award "for the most distinguished contribution to American literature for children," were also high on the list. Somehow a book entitled *Amos Fortune: Freeman,* by Elizabeth Yates, found its way into my hands. It not only won the Newbery for 1950, but also left an indelible mark on my mind and in my heart. As a matter of fact, when my wife and I were first dating, she asked me to name the best book I had ever read. Here I was, a college sophomore and budding English major being exposed to some of the world's greatest literature, and yet, without any forethought, I blurted out, "*Amos Fortune: Freeman.*" She was dumbfounded. She too had thought it the best she had ever read. No, it wasn't Shakespeare, F. Scott Fitzgerald, or Joseph Conrad, but at one point in our lives, so many years earlier, it had had an enormous impact and was a true source of inspiration.

The hero of a true story, Amos Fortune was a slave captured in Africa and, because of his stamina, brought to Massachusetts where it was thought he could survive the harsh New England winters. He was likable and intelligent and, after forty years in captivity, was allowed to purchase his freedom. He married and prospered as an accomplished tanner. He gained respect in the community and lived a life of purpose and dignity. He and his wife, Violate, are buried in a churchyard in Jaffrey, New Hampshire. To this day their graves are still marked by clearly inscribed headstones for all to see. Amos had found what we all seek in life.

I have no doubt that some of the credit for my joy in seeing Amos, a black man, triumph in the white society that enslaved him, belongs to my parents. I never heard an ethnic or racial slur uttered in our household. Not only were my parents not given to gossip, but, for whatever reasons, they respected all races and religions. They judged people by their character and work ethic, not by the color of their skin or national origin. They may have harbored some negative thoughts and biases, but they made it a point not to pass them on to me. They did the right thing.

And so the habit of reading, the best habit I ever acquired, became a permanent part of my life. Our visits to the library, Miss Grinnell's required reading and book reports, as well as my parents' regard for television as a minor but limited source of amusement, gave me a good start in the right direction.

It isn't as easy for kids today.

As Miss Grinnell was busy turning us into renaissance kids, she never lost her sense of discipline or humor. My first encounter with the former was reminiscent of that old military saw, "You never hear the one that kills you." Pow! It caught me right in the ego.

She was writing at the blackboard and, since her back was turned, I thought it a good moment to make some incredibly witty remark to one of my classmates. As she spun around, I noticed the glasses that hung from a gold chain around her neck barely had time to catch up with her sudden move. It was like the incident many years later when a drunk crossed the centerline and hit me head-on. Everything went into slow motion and, for a few seconds, I was mesmerized and fascinated, almost enchanted with the moment. Her glasses settled on her matronly bosom just as she announced for all of Waterbury to hear, "Jerry, I will see you after class." For a second I thought she was talking to Gerry Guiditta in the back of the room. But those piercing eyes were searing a hole right through my skull. The shame and embarrassment were burning my ears. I wasn't a smart-ass, just an impulsive chatterbox who had finally been outed.

At the end of the day I had to spend a half hour seated at my desk, hands folded, looking straight ahead. This would not be my last encounter with Miss Grinnell's demand for unwavering attention to the task at hand. She nailed me at least a few more times. In some respects I guess I was willing to take the risk, or maybe I was just a slow learner. Truth be told, it was probably a little of both. There was no animosity in her tone. She was simply punishing me for a wrong and trying to deter further inappropriate behavior, all of which, of course, was perfectly justified. Staying after was actually a very effective punishment for me (in spite of my occasional backsliding) and probably for my fellow miscreants as well. Thankfully, my mother was usually not aware of it because I'm sure she assumed I was just taking my time on the walk home. No matter what, I wasn't about to tell my parents. I may have been stupid, but I wasn't crazy.

Today, keeping a child after school almost requires a legislative act, and is often impossible. The loss of neighborhood schools means a kid cannot miss the bus. Even in those cases where a child lives nearby, parents usually have to be notified a day in advance that he will be staying after. If both parents are working, this may create a logistics problem. Some parents will not allow their child to stay if arrangements to pick up the child cannot be made. If a child is kept in at recess, the punishment is far less effective, especially in bad weather. And, of course, there are those parents who carp at any disciplinary action directed at their children. And so it goes. Not being able to mete out immediate and effective punishment is both frustrating and discouraging for the teacher and ultimately hurtful for the child.

When I was in school, I knew that notice of undesirable or uncooperative behavior would appear on the left side of the report card, the one without the grades: the side that had phrases like "Is attentive," "Is prompt," "Works well with others," "Is courteous." The side my parents always read first. All indications are that today's parents look at the grades first. And that alone speaks volumes.

Staying after was an effective deterrent for me because it often jettisoned my plans for after-school play. Rick and Phil would be off to the woods, and I wouldn't be able to find them. Or, as it grew dark earlier in late October or November, the football game would already have started in McNellis' backyard. And, the worst of all, on a spring afternoon, the sides would already have been chosen for a baseball game. "After school" almost invariably meant outdoor activity, which also meant that it was highly unlikely that I would find my friends sitting in their houses.

Behind my first experiences with the disciplinary measures in Miss Grinnell's class lies an extremely crucial point, one that cannot be overstated in its importance. Needless to say, a child's undivided attention is critical to his success. The seemingly minor disruptions of one child detracts from the learning of all. We learned early on that the more casual conversational chirping and interjections in our homes (though we were still taught not to interrupt adult conversation) were not acceptable in school. As the decades rolled on, in both my wife's teaching career and mine, we noticed that parents of unruly kids more and more seemed to regard their children's class disruptions as only a minor obstacle in the educational path. Those parents are wrong. Classroom interruption causes not only a loss of precious teaching time, but also produces gaps in the learning process which may never be filled.

All of what Miss Grinnell did was often accompanied with frequent smiles and a wry sense of humor. On one occasion, as she returned a graded penmanship exercise, with a smile on her lips she suggested that I think about becoming a doctor. I was flattered. My uncle Guy, the doctor, was considered the family sage. She had placed me in good company. At the same time, however, I couldn't correlate the D at the top of the paper with her remark. In fact, throughout the entire year I got straight D's in penmanship. No matter how hard I tried, the push and pull of the Palmer Method, with its graceful loops and swirls, always gave way to the cramped chicken scratchings of the Joyell Method. When I told my mother about Miss Grinnell's compliment, she laughed and asked if I had ever seen my uncle's handwriting. It would be several years later before I made the connection between poor penmanship and doctors' handwriting.

Miss Grinnell often smiled and sometimes laughed out loud at our ingenuous remarks and naïve responses, but she wasn't laughing at us. Even though she was a veteran nearing retirement, I think she never grew tired of our innocence.

I later saw that same innocence in my wife's third grade class some fifteen years later. Her school was located just across the street from mine and, since my teaching day ended a half hour before hers, I occasionally would visit her classroom. On my first visit I announced that I was the "Desk Inspector." Her students were caught off-guard and shuddered at the thought of not passing inspection. Whenever she announced the inspector's future visits, there was a flurry of activity, fearful gasps, and giddy laughter. I never actually did much inspecting, but their willingness to believe in my awesome, albeit nonexistent, powers was genuine and refreshing. Years later some of those very students became mine, and they invariably recalled their fear and trembling and their eagerness to please. They loved it.

In recently recalling those moments with my wife and some of her colleagues, all were certain the Desk Inspector would not evoke the same reaction today. They assured me that many students would not respond with even the slightest enthusiasm or concern. The nervous laughter of that class in the sixties would most likely be replaced with shrugs of indifference today. Could it be that kids so filled with a sense of self-esteem, kids who have spent so much time *being* pleased, have no eagerness to please others?

At any rate, we were eager to please our parents and Miss Grinnell. That is precisely why so much learning took place. Not only did she not pile on the homework, she didn't get us involved in monumental projects that required parental intervention. She simply kept feeding us information and building our skills through repetition, some of which was skillfully disguised as new material. And she did it in the manner she felt worked best. And the constant stream of new and varied material never stopped: we learned of the curious nesting habits of the stickleback fish; that Bolivia exports tin; the "To find, given, and method" approach to solving mathematical word problems; the notes of the musical scale; the Twenty-third Psalm; and the discovery in the early 1900s in England of what came to be known as Piltdown Man, thought to be a pre-historic relative of the British. Miss Grinnell, an inveterate anglophile, must have been very disappointed when it was learned in 1954 that Piltdown Man was a hoax. Nevertheless, she gave us a full plate. She truly enriched our first educational experience beyond the primary grades. And she marched to her own educational drumbeat as she did so.

She was able to teach as she did because parents did not question her methods. In fact, when I was a youngster, most parents barely knew our teachers. Most mothers could probably name them, but it's a safe bet that the fathers couldn't, or at least would have to think for a minute. It wasn't that they didn't care; rather, they felt our performance in the classroom, our relationship with our teachers, was our job. In other words, we were largely responsible for our own educational experience.

Miss Grinnell was also not subject to administrative wonks who are now part of a seemingly endless parade of bureaucrats that suck the life's blood and money out of school systems by making proposals to boards of education, which themselves often have a bandwagon mentality and are more interested in style than substance and truth. And now that long line of teacher wannabes leads not only to state capitals but all the way to the White House, as politicians decide that more and more standardized testing will solve the problems of our youth who seem to be learning less and less.

Thankfully, Miss Grinnell is not here today to see a group of self-styled experts turn education, which is both art and science, into a political football.

Chapter 19

There's just ae thing I cannae bear,
An' that's my conscience.

Robert Louis Stevenson

Lies sometimes have a strange way of catching up with us, as was the case with some fallout from a fourth-grade incident more than a half century after it occurred.

Ricky Lorton and I had returned to school from our lunch break, and, for reasons I cannot imagine, sneaked into our classroom about fifteen minutes before the afternoon session was to begin. It was a warm, sunny day and all the students were playing in the schoolyard, where we should have been, even though we knew students were, under any circumstances, not to be in unsupervised classrooms before the bell rang.

The hallways were dead quiet and there wasn't a teacher in sight—a perfect opportunity for an eraser fight. I have to point out that the layout of the classroom plays an important part in this misadventure. Miss Grinnell's room occupied a corner on the first floor at the front of the building. There were windows all along the front and around the corner on the side. Just beneath the side windows was the younger girls' play area. The chalkboard ran the length of the room opposite those windows. There were four erasers in the chalk trough. Three were made completely of soft felt; the other one had a hardwood top.

When the fight began, we agreed not to duck any eraser headed for the windows. We *had* to catch it. No sooner had the battle commenced, when I flung the wooden-topped eraser at Rick. Forgetting our agreement, he instinctively ducked. It flew through one of the side windows. It might have been a funny moment had it not been for the piercing screams of the girls below, who were showered with shards of glass while playing hopscotch and jacks.

We raced out of the room and mingled with our classmates in the schoolyard and agreed to tell no one.

When class resumed, we both kept a low profile and tried to look as innocent as we could. Miss Grinnell asked if anyone knew about the broken window and, thankfully, remarked how lucky it was that no one was hurt. Everyone was silent. Rick and I were relieved. And there were no repercussions, or so I remembered lo these many years.

More than fifty-one years after that eraser battle, I traveled to Waterbury to pick up my dad for Thanksgiving dinner at our home. On the half-hour return trip, I told him I had been thinking about writing a book about my childhood and the generational changes since then. I think he slightly misinterpreted my intent, gave my idea his own twist, and said, "You were a good kid in school. The only time there was a problem was when you were in fourth grade and the principal called."

That he recalled things like that at ninety-four was no surprise. His memory was legend among family members. What did shock me was that I had no such memory of a call from the principal. I questioned him. Without breaking stride, he responded, "Oh, sure. He thought you had something to do with a broken window. When I asked you, you absolutely denied it. I believed you because you were always honest. I told him the same thing and never heard any more about it." Considering how much I do remember about my childhood, I can't imagine how I could have forgotten that. But I had forgotten it, and for my father to say what he did, it had to have happened.

There I sat, an official old fart of sixty-one, and I couldn't bring myself to tell my father, over half a century later, that I must have lied to him. Instead, I just grunted at his recollection, and kept my head straight forward, pretending to watch the road and trying not to get my lengthening nose caught in the steering wheel.

It wasn't fear of his anger that kept me quiet. We had banged heads many times, man-to-man. No, it was love. I didn't want to disappoint him. I didn't want him to know that he had defended a liar all those years ago.

Dad passed away about eight months after that brief exchange. I arrived at the hospital about fifteen minutes after he died. As I approached his room, I noticed the light blinking above the door. When I walked in, I saw the curtain had been pulled around his bed and thought a nurse was tending to him since he had been doing very well the day before. I called out but got no reaction. Opening the curtain, I immediately knew he was gone. I gave him a kiss on the forehead, said a good-bye. Eyes filled with tears, I closed the curtain and headed back down the hallway toward the nurses' station to call my brother who had left about a half hour before I got there.

In the corridor a man in his forties approached. He introduced himself as the son of my father's roommate and asked if my name was Jerry. I nodded and he asked if I would like to know what my dad's last words were. I wasn't sure, but I said yes. With a little smile on his lips he repeated, "Jerry, Jerry, Jerry. Behave yourself." We both laughed. When I told family members, they laughed. When I recalled the moment while eulogizing my dad at his funeral mass, the congregation laughed. They all laughed, but I thought back to that moment in the car a few months earlier. Did he know I had lied? No matter. What really mattered, of course, was that I knew. He had given me a conscience.

Chapter 20

*Unless we get off our fat surpluses and recognize that
television in the main is being used to distract,
delude, amuse, and insulate us, then television and
those who finance it, those who look at it and those
who work at it, may see a totally different picture too
late.*

Edward R. Murrow (1958)

It was Monday, October 1, 1951, the day before my ninth birthday. They used a hand truck to bring the huge cardboard box along the walk, up the steps of the front porch, and in the door to the living room. My father pulled and my Uncle Jim guided it from the rear. They treated it with the same gentleness and care a new mother gives her first-born. There it sat, in the middle of the living room. My father deftly cut the cardboard in the right places with his Stanley knife, and it slowly fell away to reveal a seventeen-inch Philco console done in mahogany veneer. I'm surprised we didn't genuflect before this technological marvel that would bring us news and entertainment from all over the world—right there in our living room. I wonder how many Americans then suspected what kind of truly awesome power that one-eyed monster would have on our culture, thoughts, actions, feelings—our very souls.

The television was jockeyed into the corner of the living room just to the left of our grand old Stromberg-Carlson console radio, which, at that moment, was on its way to becoming an instant antique, part of America's past. The radio remained where it was for a while, but its popular stars like Bob Hope, Jack Benny, Ozzie and Harriet, and Arthur Godfrey made the leap to television in a heartbeat. My introduction to the world of entertainment, adventure, and mystery came through the radio. My mother kept it on all day. Except for a few of the fifteen-minute westerns around dinnertime, the only other listening I did was more at the subliminal level. It was always there in the background while I busied myself with something else.

When I was around seven, I began to sneak in some of the early evening shows whenever I had baby-sitters who would allow me to stay up a little later than usual. I moved beyond *Bobby Benson and the B-Bar-B Riders* to the far more intriguing worlds of *The Shadow, Mr. Keene—Tracer of Lost Persons, Gangbusters, and The FBI in Peace and War* (presented by L-A-V-A). I would lie on the living room rug, close my eyes, suspend my powers of disbelief (what little of such powers I had at that age), and fall into the embrace of that twelve-inch speaker only a few feet away from my tender ears.

Though each has its benefits, in looking back I think radio had one advantage which television, by its very nature, can't offer. Television, especially entertainment programming, inherently creates an aesthetic distance between itself and the viewer. As we watch, we, or at least our senses, are still aware that we are in a room in our house and have to live with any distractions that may be there. With radio we could close our eyes and fall into the illusion. There was no gap to bridge. To say that I saw it all in the theater of my mind is much more than a tired cliché; it is the truth. I was "watching" the action of the story, as I later did on television, but with radio I was "there." I was next to her at the front door when Henry Aldrich's mother called him; I was standing right there when Fibber McGee opened his closet and all the junk fell at our feet; I was eating at the dinner table in Ozzie and Harriet's home when wise-cracking Ricky (my contemporary) warned, "Don't mess around with me, boy." I was sitting next to Rochester as he drove Jack Benny's ancient Maxwell, chugging and spitting as it lurched down the road. I was standing below her in the street when Molly Goldberg called out her window, and, when Richard Diamond, Private Eye said he felt the "cold blue steel of a Colt .45 in my ribs," I felt that gun in my ribs (though I now question the scriptwriter about how Diamond could have known the color, caliber, and make of the gun just by feeling it). Today, all that remains of radio adventure is "Guy Noir, Private Eye" who appears every weekend on National Public Radio's *The Prairie Home Companion.* Guy's humorous adventures are only a small part of a show that continuously reminds me of how much I miss the magic of that wonderful old Stromberg-Carlson with its concentric art deco arches that looked like the door to a cathedral. Another kind of worship, I guess.

To this day, I still prefer to be in bed late at night when the Red Sox are playing on the West Coast and "see" the game on the radio. I know I'm not alone. Many of my high school students who were baseball fans agreed that they preferred to "see" the radio broadcasts of Phil Rizzuto's Yankees and Ned Martin's Red Sox. I wish they could have shared even my limited experience with the radio of my early years. I often wonder what it could have added to the power of their imaginations and their aesthetic sensibilities.

With the advent of television, radio programming had to change. The music, such as it is, remains. Though I am a child of rock and roll and will always like much of it, over the last fifteen years, with a few exceptions, most of it has become reduced to little more than cacophony. More and more I find myself listening to *The Music of Your Life,* standards from the thirties to the present that actually have melodies I can hum and lyrics I can sing—in the privacy of my car or shower of course. Most of AM radio has regrettably gone over to the news/talk format. I find "talk" radio painful. "Shout" radio might be more accurate. More heat than light, many of these programs have helped to polarize this nation. We are all apparently either conservatives or liberals. The perpetual bitching, moaning, and whining adds even more tension to a country that already has more than it can handle; and these self-important snake-oil salesmen do little more than sell simplistic answers to complex problems and laugh all the way to the bank.

With our new television set came strict orders: "Don't sit too close or you'll go blind," and "God help you if you jump on the living room floor and blow out the picture tube." Our choice of which channel to watch was decided by geography. We lived in the western section of town, which meant that the hills of Middlebury blocked the transmissions of all the big New York stations, which emanated from the top of the Empire State Building. Because television is a line-of-sight signal, we were limited to only one station, WNHC, channel six, from New Haven. It was an independent and, in those days, allowed to "cherrypick" what it wished to broadcast. We saw a variety of programs from CBS, NBC, and the now forgotten Alan B. DuMont Network.

As luck would have it, the very first thing I saw on our television was Bobby Thompson's homerun in the New York Giants-Brooklyn Dodgers playoff game on October 3, 1951. "The shot heard 'round the world," as sports reporters dubbed it. My father broke his own rule when he jumped out of his seat. I didn't reprimand him.

This was not, however, my first experience with television. About six months before we got our TV, a neighbor, Dorothy Sutton, my soon to be seventh/eighth grade English teacher, invited my brother and me to watch *Howdy Doody* with her two sons. Just before five o'clock, we would wait for the test pattern to disappear (there was no afternoon programming at that time), and be greeted with Buffalo Bob's unforgettable call to attention: "Hey, kids! What time is it?" The kids in the Peanut Gallery would cry out in unison, "It's Howdy Doody time!"

Truthfully, I was less than moderately amused, probably because I was a bit too old. Flub-a-dub, Dilly Dally, Mr. Bluster, and Chief Thunder Thud (Cowabunga!) just didn't work for me. And at the risk of seeming uncharitable, I found Clarabelle to be nothing but annoying. Good taste prevents me from saying what I would have done with his horn. There simply wasn't any magic for me there.

I was, however, just the right age for my next viewing experience. I became an official child of the Television Age a few months later when I visited my cousin Jim's house to see *The Lone Ranger*. What captured me then was neither the action nor the plot; rather, it was the essence of the medium itself, the spectacle of it all. The immediacy, the *now* of early television gave so much of it a vibrancy and import that far outweighed the content of the shows themselves.

I, of course, was fascinated by the Masked Man and Tonto, but what gave the experience its unrelenting magnetism was a wonderful introduction that conquered my senses. How could I not be completely enraptured by the majesty of *The William Tell Overture* and by the larger-than-life voice that beckoned me to "return with us now to those thrilling days of yesteryear." Add to these the visual images of the Lone Ranger rearing on Silver, his "fiery horse with the speed of light," and it's not difficult to see how a youngster could so easily fall prey to the overwhelming sights and sounds of this new technological wonder. The ho-hum plot of what followed was of little importance.   All I knew was that I was witnessing an event, not just a TV show.

Even the evening news, *The Camel Caravan*, caught my imagination and raised my blood pressure. John Cameron Swayze, who, as most Americans did not know, was an actor hired to read the news, delivered it with such a sense of urgency that even the most mundane story became gripping.

The storm of the news was followed by the calm of *Kukla, Fran, and Ollie.* Puppeteer Burr Tillstrom and hostess Fran Allison provided fifteen minutes of gentleness and warmth. I could sense but not fully understand the subtle irony in the wordplay between Fran and the characters. Kukla's voice of reason juxtaposed to the gentle evil of Beulah Witch, the pompousness of Colonel Crackie, the lovable dumbness of Oliver J. Dragon, and the complete innocence of his adorable niece, Dolores Dragon, all played off Miss Allison's maternal guidance and wisdom. I especially liked those moments when Miss Allison would break up (like most in those days, the show was live). Instead of bursting the bubble, those moments actually enhanced the "reality" of the show. For youngsters, and some oldsters, this simple fifteen-minute piece of magic would still work today.

Like most Americans, I quickly became used to this new miracle and, after the thrill wore off, the reality became clear. Some shows were entertaining, some weren't. *I Remember Mama* was a strong and intelligent show that dealt with a loving family and their everyday problems—a formula that will always be successful. It was followed by *The Life of Reilly*, a run-of-the-mill sitcom that offered the mindless adventures of a bumbling father. That too will always be with us.

I Love Lucy was so popular that my parents allowed my brother and me to stay up until 8:30 on Monday nights, a half hour past our regular school night bedtime. The entire show hinged on Lucille Ball's gift for physical comedy. It worked well then. I'm not so sure it would succeed today, whereas I believe the sophisticated comedy of Sid Caesar, Bob and Ray, and Ernie Kovaks still would.

Good or bad, most television was harmless escapism designed to help people relax at the end of the day. And most families watched it together. That fact alone gave it a value beyond the quality of the programs themselves.

Where television succeeded then (and now) was in its power to do what radio simply couldn't do. Whereas radio required us to use our imagination to be drawn into the story, some things are difficult to imagine. They must be seen. Television offers events whose beauty, power, or horror can only be fully realized through visual images. Disney gave us the wonders and beauty of nature on Sunday evenings, and the network news departments gave us the raw power of early morning nuclear explosions from Yucca Flats, Nevada, and Bikini Atoll in the South Pacific. But, for me, the most powerful images came on Saturday afternoons when my dad and I watched *Victory at Sea*. The war I saw in those programs was not as clean and neat as *The Sands of Iwo Jima* or *The Steel Helmet*, which I had seen at the Tower Theater on other Saturday afternoons. I saw men floundering in the ocean after their ships had been sunk, refugees with looks of terror on their faces, cold-blooded executions, and the aftermath of the holocaust. My father explained and I watched, mouth agape, eyes wide open. I was too young to dwell on what I saw and doing so would not have been healthy for a youngster. But I always remembered it. Such images should never be forgotten.

Early entertainment television was anything but realistic. Mothers decked out in earrings, pearls, and heels, and dads in shirts and ties were not part of the world I knew. And always the twin beds. I thought this must be the way rich people slept since my working class parents could apparently afford only a double bed.

That less than real picture was slow to change. Rob and Laura Petrie (*The Dick VanDyke Show*) were still in twin beds in the early sixties. I do recall, however, that Ozzie would occasionally dress down to a cardigan. But by the end of the sixties *Rowan and Martin's Laugh-in* brought us the Dirty Old Man and was awarding the Fickle Finger of Fate to deserving individuals.

By the mid-seventies *Happy Days* did touch lightly on sexual issues, and the frisky and bawdy Sue Ann Nivens, the Happy Homemaker on *The Mary Tyler Moore Show*, was less than subtle in her pursuit of Mary's boss, Lou Grant. Still, this was essentially wink-wink humor that was hardly titillating and would fly over the head of any kid.

The early eighties brought cable and with it the opportunity, especially for the premium channels, to go more than a step further with graphic sex and violence. But, of course, the other channels had to compete for viewers, so the bar was lowered. The networks, the big boys on the block, were beginning to feel the crunch, so they jumped on the bandwagon that was headed down the Primrose Path. The research is simple. Turn on the TV and you'll get the picture.

Meanwhile, back at the ranch house in suburbia, kids were being allowed to stay up later and later. And parents were placing television sets in the bedrooms of Junior and Missy. To this day, I cannot think of one good reason why parents would allow kids their own TV sets—not one.

My parents controlled the television. On weekdays it was not turned on until after dinner. When we soon graduated to three channels, they chose the programs. This would explain why *The Firestone Hour*, an early primetime show devoted primarily to operatic music, encouraged me to retire to my bedroom and either read or do my homework.

Every time I think TV has reached the lowest limits, it lowers the bar again. It's not prudery. It's a matter of good taste, and screwing up kids' heads even more than they already are. I certainly don't want government censorship. That could be even more dangerous. In a speech delivered in 1961, FCC Chairman Newton Minnow said, "When television is bad, nothing is worse. I invite you to sit down in front of your television set when your station goes on the air . . . and keep your eyes glued to that set until the station goes off. I can assure you that you will observe a vast wasteland."

The opening quote for this chapter was made by legendary news reporter Edward R. Murrow in 1958. Both that and the one above implicitly ask the same question: how far will it go? More than forty years later we still have to ask: How much longer do we want our kids to wallow in this cesspool of gratuitous titillation and violence? The answer lies in how much we respect ourselves.

Television is driven by ratings, and ratings convert to advertising dollars. All we have to do, each of us by ourselves, is write a letter, or send an e-mail and tell someone "we're mad as hell and we're not going to take it anymore." And then we have to take control of our television sets and not watch, and not let ourselves be fooled.

The other night we caught the opening of a seven o'clock rerun of one of the most popular sit-coms. The mother was desperately looking for her "diaphragm." My wife rhetorically asked, "How do parents explain what that word means when their ten-year-old asks?" All the writers had to do was be a little more subtle, but they and the producers knew we wouldn't object.

If we love our kids, we will write that letter.

Chapter 21

You win some,
You lose some,
And some get rained out.

Anonymous

She was like a one-eyed jack in class. We never got to see the other side of Miss Fitzgerald's handsome but inexpressive face. She wore that mask of which I spoke earlier. Don't misunderstand. She wasn't an ogre or anything close to that. It was just that she didn't bring any enthusiasm or emotion to the show. I have always had two absolute requirements for teachers: know your stuff backwards and forwards, and teach it with passion. A sense of humor also wouldn't hurt.

Miss Fitzgerld was my teacher for fifth grade, as well as for seventh grade English and eighth grade U.S. History. She did her job. She faithfully covered the material and graded all our work, while maintaining an even, if not warm and fuzzy, classroom decorum. Still, they weren't classes that I looked forward to.

She was young—I would guess around thirty-five—a very attractive woman and a stylish dresser, especially fond of scarves. Her look suggested something other than her classroom persona. What made the situation even more confusing was that, quite by accident, I did catch a peek at the other side of Miss Fitzgerald when I once had to deliver a message to the Teachers' Room. It was the only place where teachers could escape the students' eyes, usually when the music or art teacher took over the class. I was instructed to knock and enter only if invited to do so. Miss Finnan came to the door, took the note, read it, and asked me to wait for a reply. I stood just inside the door of this L-shaped inner sanctum but could see Miss Fitzgerald just around the corner. She was engaged in animated conversation, gesticulating, laughing, (I think I even saw a cigarette), the portrait of a happy person loaded with personality. I was dumbstruck. I had never seen that face in class, and I never would.

Our desks faced the blackboard and her desk was to our left at the rear of the class. Because she spent most of her time teaching from there, and we had our faces buried in our books, there was little eye contact. When she called on us, it was merely a disembodied voice from the back of the room.

We pretty much had to supply our own motivation. We all were aware that school was our job, an important job. Nobody had to say it. Still, her manner made the learning process a little more difficult than it had to be. I think she became too comfortable in her small, protected enclave behind us. Or maybe she just wasn't happy doing what she was doing. Maybe she was one of many women who, years earlier, were caught in that maze that led to so few career choices. I neither expected nor wanted her to employ that sugary, patronizing tone some used as if they were talking to a puppy in the pet store. But our enthusiasm for what we were doing could have been raised several degrees if she would have just occasionally left the safety of Fort Fitzgerald and looked directly at us as she asked a question, or just walked alongside our desks and took just a few seconds of personal interest in what we were doing. Some constructive criticism, a little praise, or even a touch on the shoulder can go a long way in making a little kid believe he and his work have import beyond the purely academic.

There was, however, a small moment in the hallway I have never forgotten. I was in eighth grade and we were lining up to leave for the day. We would pair up in no particular order and walk down the stairs to the first floor. Our march out of the school, at both lunch time and at the end of the day, was always accompanied by a student playing "American Patrol," "The Marine Hymn," or some other march on the upright piano situated in the foyer.

As we were waiting for the classes in front of us to file out, I felt a slight tug on my shirt collar. Boys had taken to wearing their collars up at that time. I turned to see Miss Fitzgerald turning mine down. She then gently patted that portion of my shirt. I bristled at first. "You're not my mother," I thought. But then I saw a warm smile on her face accompanied by unmistakable eye contact. I said nothing. I was not about to start a war over such a minor incident, especially not with a teacher. But those first reactions melted away when I thought that what she had done had a maternal touch. I don't think it was just another of those moments when teachers, adults, or society demanded absolute but unreasonable conformity to some unwritten standard. No, I think it was another glimpse of the other side of Miss Fitzgerald's face. Maybe she was trying to tell me not to blindly conform to the latest fad, or maybe she was just trying to tell me I looked better with my collar down. Whichever it was, I liked the fact that she took a moment to recognize me as a person, as more than the back of a head facing the blackboard.

A few months later we saw her pull into a parking spot in a brand new black Ford Thunderbird. Her "cool" quotient, especially in the eyes of the young boys who were rapidly becoming part of the car cult of the fifties, rose meteorically. And I think I finally had Miss Fitzgerald figured out.

Chapter 22

I don't like work—no man does—but I like what is in work—the chance to find yourself.

Joseph Conrad

I'm not sure if I found work or it found me, but in the spring of fifth grade I was handed my first regular assignment of household chores. As we finished dinner one evening, my father suggested that my brother and I were old enough to accept responsibility for a couple of household duties. Every evening after dinner my brother, Al, was to sweep the linoleum and hardwood floors of the kitchen and dining area. My new job was to dry the dishes. We didn't have a dishwasher and never would. Mom washed and I dried, an arrangement that would continue until I was married and left home.

I was also given the task of mowing the lawn. I was strong enough to push our new reel mower, which Dad bought at Sears, the source of every tool in our garage. After a workday in a hot brass factory, I'm sure my father didn't look forward to coming home to yard work. But more than that, he was a strong believer in the work ethic. He was a very hard worker, as was my mother, as were most Americans then and still are now. He expected the same from me. When he "suggested" the lawn needed mowing, I knew that I had better have it done before the old Buick came chugging up Circuit Avenue that afternoon.

I was never paid for my chores. We were a family and that meant we all chipped in. The same attitude applied to shoveling snow. If it snowed overnight, he would clear the driveway before he left for work at six in the morning. I was expected to do the rest before he got home. I was not to let my mother help out, though she often tried. There was no debate, no discussion, no whining. These were my jobs and I did them.

Not only was I not paid for my chores, but I also did not get an allowance. I was given those things I needed, along with small change now and then, but if I wanted a new baseball glove, a squirt gun, or a vanilla Coke from the soda fountain at Charlie's Drugstore, I had to find a way to support myself.

As luck would have it, an elderly couple named Bloodgood moved into a small cape two houses around the corner. One evening in late spring of that year I knocked on their door and Mr. Bloodgood answered. I offered to cut his lawn. He said he would like to speak to my parents first, probably because I was so young. The next evening he appeared at our front door, spoke with my father, and I got the job.

His front lawn was quite small. His backyard was never landscaped and was little more than a rock-strewn weed patch. I completed my first mowing in thirty minutes, using our push mower. My new employer asked what I thought would be fair pay. I had no idea. As I was to later learn, he was a plain-talking frugal Yankee with a '37 Packard in the garage. His compensation offer was in keeping with his lifestyle. "How about a penny a minute?" he said. I nodded and he handed me a quarter and a nickel. I was satisfied and proud that my efforts had earned a couple of sodas and a Fifth Avenue candy bar. But the real bonus came when I pushed the mower into our garage. My dad asked how it went. I told him. He beamed.

After a couple of years my pay and responsibilities grew. I became their factotum—their handyman. I shoveled snow, raked leaves, trimmed the shrubbery, cleaned the basement, and moved furniture. Age had taken its toll on both of them, so I did what they no longer could. I even cleared the weed patch behind their house, spread loam that Mr. Bloodgood had ordered for the job, seeded, rolled, and watered. My father told me what to do and supplied all the tools, but I did all the work myself. When the lawn came in, I didn't just mow and trim it, I manicured it .

By the time I turned sixteen, I had outgrown the job. I was playing football in the fall and running track in the spring and had picked up a regular part-time job as a stack-boy in the city library, which I worked between sports and during the summer months. The problem was the elderly couple had become dependent upon me. I decided to take care of their property *pro bono*. I just couldn't bring myself to knock on the door when I finished shoveling or mowing. When I did see either of them, they never failed to thank me. I knew their situation and they knew I did, and learned that giving, much more than getting, boosts self-esteem.

Around my freshman year of college both passed away. I worked for nothing in their last years because I had always liked them. There was nothing artificial about them. They were good, simple people. They had given me the opportunity to learn responsibility, to work independently, to manage my time, to use a little ingenuity, and to have a vanilla Coke at Charlie's Drugstore.

There were other jobs. During the winters I shoveled any driveway I could. It was the toughest work but the most lucrative. In the summers, whenever we could figure out how to make the three-mile trip, a few of us caddied at Waterbury Country Club, a fine Donald Ross layout listed among the one hundred oldest courses in America. We made between two and three dollars a round, but, for a kid not much taller than a golf bag, trudging up and down a hilly course on a hot summer's day was a tough way to earn a buck.

Golf carts have replaced caddies at most golf clubs. In fact, many of my boyhood jobs have been eliminated by snow blowers, power mowers, and lawn services. At the same time, two-parent income has apparently given many kids enough spending money not to have a need to pursue the few jobs that are out there. Paper routes have gone begging, finding a baby sitter is tough, and getting a youngster to help out with the lawn is nearly impossible, at least in our typical middle-class neighborhood. I must add one eye-opening observation. When I was thirteen, the minimum wage was about seventy-five cents an hour. Those who could afford it usually paid about two dollars for a lawn that took an hour to mow, which, coincidentally, is exactly how long it takes to mow our lawn. On those rare occasions now when I need someone to mow it, I pay twenty-five to thirty dollars. If I were to pay only today's minimum wage, or even double that, the lawn would be over the top of the house before I could find help. And, the final irony is that still, at a rate of twenty-five dollars an hour, finding a youngster who is willing to do the work is no small challenge. With fewer opportunities and less need, kids lose the chance to develop the kind of work habits that last a lifetime.

The memories of some boyhood job experiences can last a lifetime as well. What proved to be the most exciting, revealing, and memorable moments were the one-day stints we got when the circuses came to town. As expected, each offered sideshows intended for a general audience, but one provided a memorable show we never expected

In the summer after fifth grade the Barnum and Bailey/Ringling Brothers circus train rolled into Waterbury. We knew we had to be at the railroad spur on the huge vacant lots across from American Brass at around 5:00 A.M. to pick up a job and earn free tickets. With less than a mile to walk, Phil and I arrived on time and were given the task of carrying buckets of water to where the elephants were tethered. The job was both difficult and dangerous. A full bucket of water is quite a burden for a ten year old. We had to pour it into a huge tub only a few feet away from these great beasts. They were truly impressive and, thankfully, stood quietly as we did our job. Looking back, I remember a sad stoicism in their eyes, as if they knew the rest of their lives would be spent in captivity.

All the kids who worked were given tickets to the sideshow, not to the big top as we expected. For me, that disappointment was followed by an even bigger one—the sideshow itself. They all were there: the fat lady, the world's tallest man, the smallest man, the tattooed man, and the bearded lady. I thought all looked sad, and felt guilty that I was there staring at them. I expected amusement but left there feeling only a strange emptiness.

My only other circus experience was quite different. In the summer of the next year, the Clyde Beatty/Coleman Brothers circus, much smaller than Barnum and Bailey, came to town and set up in the parking lot next to Municipal Stadium, less than a mile from my house. Phil and I arrived just after dawn. We were assigned the task of carrying the ropes, pipes, and huge stakes that were used to hold up the big top. The job took most of the morning, but we were rewarded with tickets to both the afternoon and evening shows under the big tent.

Some of the roustabouts liked our efforts and apparently adopted us as their mascots for the day. They invited us to eat with them, so we decided we wouldn't go home between shows. Our parents, of course, had no way of knowing this.

It grew dark and as the evening show was wrapping up, somehow Phil and I became separated. The big top had cleared out and I aimlessly wandered around the grounds looking for my companion. It was late and I suspected we were already in trouble. As suddenly as he disappeared, he reappeared, excited and out of breath. In trying to find his way back from the restrooms, he apparently had walked through the narrow area between the stadium proper and the trailers that were used by the performers as sleeping and dressing quarters—and undressing quarters. He led me to a quiet dark spot behind the trailer used by the female acrobats. For some reason it had large windows, probably because it was used as living quarters. He told me to be quiet and just watch. I did as he said, and no sooner had he spoken than a comely blonde walked by the window. And then another. Before long the traffic grew heavy—and naked. Phil had stumbled upon their dressing room, a bit of serendipity for two young boys. I had never before seen female nudity in the flesh. Phil and I looked at each other and I can only assume I was wearing the same stupid grin he was. I was reminded of those days in Pat's barbershop many years earlier and that calendar up on the wall, only this was the real thing and I was several years older. Embarrassment, guilt, and titillation were all tugging at my emotions, not to mention the fear of being caught, and also not to mention the larger fear of being killed by my parents for being out way past my curfew.

We reluctantly decided to start for home. Just as we emerged from behind the trailers and headed toward Watertown Avenue, my father's green Buick pulled into the parking lot. As we both hopped into the front seat, I noticed my father was smiling. Was he just being Mr. Nice Guy for Phil's benefit? Would the hammer fall later?

He shifted into first and we chugged off into the night for the short ride home. It was 10:30. We had been gone since six that morning. I was starting to perspire profusely, and it wasn't because of the late-night August heat.

Dad asked us if we had seen things we liked. "Oh yeah," we sang out in two-part harmony—Phil's voice had risen an octave or two. I was sitting next to my father so I kept a straight face. Phil was doing his best to smother his infectious cackle and kept shooting his elbow into my ribs.

When we pulled up at Phil's house just up the hill from ours, his mother came out to greet us. It was then I discovered why my father wore that big smile of amusement. Somehow our parents had gotten the notion that we had decided to run off with the circus. Now, relieved, they saw only our boyish desire for adventure, and had a good laugh. Phil and I just smiled.

We said goodnight and headed down the hill for home. There would be no hammer that night. My father was happy that we had the ambition to seek work, and he was genuinely amused by his mistaken assumption that we were going to run off. I think he was caught up in a wistful moment about his own boyhood dreams.

I went straight to bed and quickly fell asleep. And I never told him about the unexpected sideshow we had witnessed that night.

Chapter 23

Behold the child, by Nature's kindly law,
Pleas'd with a rattle, tickled with a straw . . .
Alexander Pope

The first toys I remember were my soldier doll, Buster, and my Panda, aptly named Panda. The first toy I actually remember playing with was a very large button. My father took a thick piece of cotton string and ran it through one hole then back through another, creating a loop about a foot and a half long with the button in the middle. He had me place the ends of the loop around the middle finger of each hand and then he moved my hands in and out as if I were playing an accordion. The button would begin to spin so quickly that it emitted a humming sound much like that of an angry bumblebee. I'm sure it was one of those legacies of those who grew up the impoverished children of immigrants who knew little or nothing of the world of toys, other than what some clever parent could fashion out of simple household materials. It's difficult for me, probably impossible for today's kids, to imagine that on one Christmas morning my dad's only gift was an orange. That's all.

I never had many toys, and those that I did receive came only at Christmas or on my birthday. My early years brought a View Master, a bulldozer, cowboy guns, a tricycle (does that qualify as a toy?), Chinese checkers set, Lincoln logs, and a box of Tinker Toys. I also played with my mother's pots and pans. Those, and some coloring and picture books, just about cover my first eight years. I'm sure I've forgotten a couple of others, but the fact that I remember so few says enough.

As I got a bit older, I graduated to things I could use outside of the house—sporting goods like a fishing rod, a peewee football, a baseball and glove. For indoor activities I had several paint-by-the-numbers kits. I loved the smell of the oil paints, and though there was no true artistry involved, seeing a picture emerge from my assiduous efforts was exciting and encouraged me to try to paint something from a sketch of my own with the leftover paint. They were good rainy-day projects.

I had several jigsaw puzzles, but the one I liked most was the map of the United States. The capital of each state was printed in bold letters on each piece. I did the puzzle so often that the pieces began to delaminate and finally fell apart. My repeated attempts taught me all the states and their capitals, but I admit it was four percent easier in those days. There were, after all, only forty-eight. The only other indoor toy I received was truly spectacular and, as I later learned, at least partially the result of an ulterior motive.

Sometime in the summer of 1952 an A.C.Gilbert catalog appeared on the coffee table in our living room. Gilbert was the New Haven manufacturer of American Flyer model trains as well as Erector and chemistry sets. The fact that this handsomely illustrated, four-colored catalog just popped out of the blue never even occurred to me. All I knew was that it was there, and it worked its magic. I wanted those trains. I even pretended to operate an imaginary transformer as I knelt at the coffee table and watched steam engines and diesels, visible only to me, race around the tracks. Once or twice my dad asked if I liked what I saw, and then walked away with a smug look on his face.

A few months later, early on Christmas morning, I sprinted to the living room to find that my thousands of "Hail Marys" and "Our Fathers" had been answered. There on the living room floor was an oval of tracks on a simulated gravel roadbed and a steam engine with a red mail car and three green passenger cars with silhouettes of riders in the windows. The transformer was already plugged in. I pushed the "on" button and carefully dialed up the power. The tiny headlight of this perfect model of the huge mechanical beasts I had stood next to on the tracks of Waterbury's train station came on, and the engine slowly began to move. Tiny clouds of pungent smoke puffed out of the stack in perfect syncopation with the chugging of this answered prayer. My journey of several years into model railroading had begun.

The journey of another little boy had also begun: that same little boy whose only gift so many Christmases ago was an orange. The catalog that magically appeared; the trains that had been bought two years before I was born, as I later learned; our frequent trips to Waterbury's train station: it was all a set-up. Dad had not only engendered an interest in trains in his son, he had been able to give himself the kind of toy that didn't even exist when he was a child. The number of trains and the size of the layout grew over the next few years, but my interest waned when high school activities limited my time for hobbies. Dad continued to refine and rework layouts. I was glad for him, but years later, I felt both sad and guilty that I hadn't kept up my interest. In a small way, it seemed as if I had abandoned him in something he might have wished to share a little longer with a son who was growing up—maybe too fast.

I still have the trains, all carefully wrapped and waiting for my grandsons, Luke and Colby. When I assembled them on Christmas Eve 1977 for my own boys, I hadn't considered that we had taken them to see Star Wars some five months earlier. Unfortunately, on that Christmas morning, it became clear that much of the romance of model railroading was lost on them. My fascination with trains was not going to be theirs. My eight-and six- year-old sons were true children of the Space Age. I wrapped up the trains and stored them in the furnace room where they await an imagination willing to take a journey back in time. Among the next Christmas' gifts for my boys was the *Millennium Falcon*.

There were other toys to amuse us, but our interest in them was short-lived. There were pea-shooters (navy beans worked best), but there wasn't much we could do with them, except maybe choke on a pea. Squirt guns were great fun but only when used surreptitiously in school. The smallest one I ever had was called the Wee Gee. It was a black, futuristic, Buck Rogers kind of weapon that had no trigger guard and was small enough to be concealed in a young boy's hand. Not only could I blast a friend in the crowded schoolyard and not be discovered, but I also was able to get off a shot or two at the young lady of my choice in the hallway.

When boys begin to develop even the slightest interest in the opposite sex, it's required that, at least part of the time, they act like complete idiots. I was clearly holding my own in that regard. A couple of enterprising girls, however, were, as usual, one step ahead of the boys and got the idea to load their water guns with cheap perfume. Their devastating retaliations put an end to my license to squirt and effectively ended my interest in water pistols.

Of course, none of this behavior went unnoticed, and teachers confiscated scores of guns, but we weren't about to tell our parents. How would I respond when my dad asked, "What the hell were you doing with a squirt gun in school?"

Today, however, as my wife, a fourth grade teacher often notes, that when forbidden electronic games are confiscated, some parents often show up not only to reclaim their child's game, but also to give the teacher a lecture about infringing on students' rights.

The last pure, big-selling toy that was part of my childhood was the yo-yo, although the incredibly successful hoola hoop was not far behind. The yo-yo was an overnight success, especially with the boys. It was easy to carry, could be used at recess, and offered a challenge to those who wanted to learn the skills necessary for tricks such as the loop-the-loop, walk-the-dog, and, my favorite, rock-the-baby-in-the-cradle. Duncan yo-yo owned the market. I had one with a simple stripe on the side. The top-of-the-line yo-yo had four faux diamonds imbedded in the stripe, but a kid had to be very good if he were going to flash this model, usually wielded only by masters. Such was the popularity of this simple toy that there were exhibitions and contests at the Tower Theater before the Saturday matinees. And then, just as I had mastered many of the tricks, which I can still perform, the yo-yo, like so many fads, disappeared as quickly as a summer shower. What I find interesting about such phenomena begs the question: Why doesn't the next crop of kids, just a couple of years younger, pick up on the fad that captured so many of us? Is it because something new has caught their fancy, or is there a more complex answer? In any event, I have none.

The mix of kids and toys today is at once both telling and somewhat disheartening. Too many children have far too many toys, and some of them are a danger to their intellectual, emotional, and physical development. The correlation between video games and dangerously increasing obesity in children has already been well documented. And it doesn't take much of a stretch to see the effect that the graphic violence in so many videos has had on youngsters, especially boys.

Two other "toys" that have been placed in kids' hands are the cell phone and the computer. Both are used by the youngest for little more than their own amusement.   Cell phones are largely unnecessary, distracting, and promote needless conversations, something they surely don't need any more of. Time spent doodling on a computer by youngsters could be far better used reading a book or getting some exercise. As two colleagues of mine who, for decades, taught computer sciences at the high school level point out, a computer is simply a tool. At the K-8 level students should continue to develop and refine their reading, writing, and math skills, as well as their fundamental knowledge of the sciences, social studies, arts, and music. They will pick up their computer skills later—and quickly—just as many of their parents have, they who had never even seen a computer in school.

Another issue is the sheer volume of toys that so many kids have. My observations tell me it has created an I-want-therefore-I-shall-get mentality. Many, perhaps the majority of today's parents, respond to their children's buying impulses as if they were given a command from on high. With the enormous spending power that has developed over the last fifty years, we have fallen prey to the mistaken notion that an abundance of things will bring a sense of well-being. And it seems we have redoubled our efforts to perpetuate this myth in our children and thereby double their disappointment when they discover life runs much deeper than the acquisition of things. Children who have been given all they want often carry that attitude into school. With a sense of entitlement already well established, it's not that great a leap to understand how many students feel they should get the grade they want. This is no secret to veteran teachers, and it applies to today's students at all levels of education.

This is one area where the well-meaning parent can blunt some of the societal forces that vie for our kids' minds. With a little self-restraint and some common sense, we can still show them we love them by giving them fewer toys and, when we do, making sure they're the right ones.

Chapter 24

Therefore all seasons shall be sweet to thee . . .
Samuel Taylor Coleridge

With few exceptions, I was past the world of toys after fifth grade, though I will allow that model trains are for kids of all ages. Then, as I do today, whenever I hear the word play, I think of outdoor activities. The gifts I most appreciated were my bike, a fishing rod, a pair of ice skates, a football and a baseball glove. As the seasons brought different weather conditions, we effortlessly changed gears and moved on to different activities. Being confined to the house was simply an unacceptable option, and only the most extreme conditions, a driving rain, below zero temperatures, or a rare hurricane, would keep us indoors. Life was to be lived outdoors.

The fall brought tackle football in McNellis' huge backyard and Halloween. Trick-or-treating in those days was not dangerous. We didn't have to worry about some sick mind slipping razor blades into apples or poisoning candy. The chill October night, the excitement of creating just the right costume, the neighbors pretending not to know who we were, and enough candy to make a dentist's heart leap with joy made it a truly wonderful evening. Left on our own, we roamed the surrounding neighborhoods in complete safety.

While our Halloweens were absolutely safe, our football games were another story. We had little or no protective equipment. Wearing several sweatshirts provided our only safeguard. On one occasion, however, we had a helmet. The good news was it would give the ball carrier some protection if he caught a knee in the head. The bad news was that, in the huddle, we gave the helmet to the kid who was going to carry the ball. This gave the defenders a pretty good idea of whom they should key on. After little or no gains, and several crushing tackles, we got smart and went to mostly a passing game.

Winter snows were a godsend. It wasn't a matter of "snow" days off from school. We had very few of those because we attended neighborhood schools. We walked and the teachers all used tire chains in the worst conditions, a must with Waterbury's hills.

Fortunately, I lived next to one of those hills. Wayland Avenue provided a steep, one thousand-foot run that carried so little traffic that safety, where sledding was concerned, was only a minor consideration. The public works crews were slow to plow it, almost intentionally it now seems. Once the first snow had accumulated, it seemed as if a signal had sounded. The hill was suddenly alive with kids. I immediately grabbed some steel wool and polished the runners of my long Flexible Flyer, and then raced to a scene   that had none of the quaintness of a Currier and Ives print which usually gave us a portrait of children, seated on their sleds, sliding down gentle slopes. Belly-floppers all, each of us was trying to reach Mach One as we raced down the treacherous hill. Sometimes we would tie three or four sleds closely together and then tether a final, smaller sled with a ten-foot rope. As the lead sleds carved S-shaped turns down the hill, the last sled would be whipped to god-awful speeds. The kid who braved that ride would sometimes not be found until the spring thaw. Night and day we would ride the hill and then repeat the long climb to the top, always buoyed by the thought of yet one more run. It was a mixture of gut-wrenching thrills and vigorous exercise.

When there was no snow to slide on, there was ice to skate on. A couple of months after I left the streets of the North End, I was introduced to ice skating while spending a winter weekend at my Aunt Lena's house about a mile up the road from ours. My mother had given me an old pair of her skates that looked like a cross between figure and hockey skates. A small pond across from my aunt's was abuzz with boys a year or two older. I strapped on the skates, and repeatedly stood up and fell down, while they adroitly whipped around the ice intensely engaged in a pick-up hockey game. They saw my ineptness as an opportunity, handed me a push broom and a catcher's mask, and pronounced me the goalie. They placed a large rock on either side of me and told me I could do anything I wanted to stop the puck, which was, fortunately, only an empty soda can.

There I was, legs splayed, push broom at the ready. It was fun, but I wanted to stand up and move about as they did. That wasn't going to happen that day or the next. But like so many other things in life, perseverance paid off. A few weeks later I found myself standing upright and unsteadily pushing myself along. I got a new pair of hockey skates the following Christmas and became good enough to snatch the girls' knitted hats from their heads at the Gunlots, a couple of nearby baseball fields that were flooded for the skating season.

There were seventeen skating areas in the city at that time, all listed on a huge sign on the city green; such was the popularity of this great winter pastime. So many of my classmates skated that our enthusiasm even prompted us to bring shovels and clear the area in the event that it had snowed.

When we reached sixth grade, most of us were allowed to skate for a couple of hours in the evening (the area was lighted). After we were thoroughly frozen and exhausted, a small herd of boys and girls would head for the Litchfield Farm Shop, a nearby dairy bar with a touch of class. Hot chocolate was about all we could afford, but the girls, whom we had just spent a couple of hours harassing, the beginning signs of the dating ritual, always appreciated the clumsy gestures of young boys trying to become young gentlemen.

Skating wasn't a passing fad. I later graduated to a pair of Canadian Flyer figure skates and skated for years with my wife. Many years later, we skated on the rink at Rockefeller Center in New York City with our boys. I don't see kids around my part of the world skating much anymore. They're missing not only the benefits of great exercise, but also a good socialization experience—and one more thing that only skaters can appreciate. There are few moments more pleasurable in life than taking off those skates after a couple of hours and slipping into a comfortable pair of shoes. And that's a fact.

Spring was probably the worst season for outdoor play. We were pretty much placed in a holding pattern. The weather gods teased us with a couple of beautiful March days, then the winds and bone-chilling cold would return, often with heavy, wet snow. April was equally fickle. All the leaves were not out until mid-May and even then the warm weather was not a guarantee. Although spring in New England is actually our shortest season, the baseball gloves were already oiled (with neat's-foot oil) and ready for a catch, and the fishing reels were filled with line in anticipation of searching for brookies in the local streams.

After the crisp autumn air, redolent with the smell of burning leaves, the postcard- perfect blanket of a gentle snowfall in the dead of winter, and the promise and resurrection of budding life in the spring, came the summer, and that, as no other, is the season made for kids. It was never a matter of finding something to do, but it was our obligation to go out and do it.

When we weren't playing a baseball game, we actively sought some kind of project, exploration, or adventure. Some doings were risky, if not downright dangerous; others were surprisingly simple, even moderately productive. In our exploration of the huge acreage just above my house, we found a large meadow of high grass and scrub surrounded by heavily treed land. In the middle of this open area we discovered several enormous blueberry bushes. I don't know if they had been planted by someone long before, or were the result of seed from bird droppings. And I still can't explain why birds hadn't gotten to them before we did, but each year the branches drooped low, heavy with plump berries. Phil and I learned to work fast and efficiently. After a full morning's effort, we would usually fill two full buckets.

When I brought them home to be washed, my mother's face lit up. Her favorite dessert was blueberry pie, but what I favored were her unmatchable blueberry muffins. She would take what she needed, and I would pack the rest into quart baskets and sell them door-to-door around the neighborhood for twenty-five cents, a bargain even in those days. Phil and I, along with our mothers, were proud that our ingenuity and effort produced one of those rare moments where everyone came away a winner.

We spent countless hours exploring the nearby woods and created projects for ourselves that made little sense but were fun. With our Boy Scout hatchets we often cut down two-or-three-inch saplings, lashed them together with bark stripped from birches, and made lean-tos, which we planned to use but never did. I once climbed a huge poplar next to one of our construction sites and tied an American flag to the very top. I don't know why I did it, and I'm equally sure no one ever saw it. I think we fancied ourselves frontiersmen and tried to emulate those who had settled this country. Maybe there was a bit of James Fenimore Cooper's Natty Bumppo in many a young boy then.

There were other less sensible and far more dangerous doings in our quest for summer excitement. On more than one occasion Phil, Rick, Jim Sullivan, and I ventured down to the confluence of the west branch and main flow of the very polluted Naugatuck River (since then made nearly pristine by environmental efforts), which met at a dump often frequented by hobos and other less savory types. I have no idea how we found it, but mischievous boys seem to have a knack for finding such places. One of the others had a B-B gun (my parents never caved in to my pleadings), and Phil and I had slingshots we had purchased from an ad in Field and Stream. They were made of metal, cost $2.50 each, and came from the Tinker Manufacturing Company in LaPierre, Michigan. I don't know why I remember all that. Maybe because it is still in a drawer in my basement, one of those pieces of our past that seems to follow us no matter where we go. Or, it could be the irony of being allowed to have a slingshot, which could hurl a ball bearing through a Sherman tank, but not a B-B gun. I knew then, however, as I do now, that there are many undesirable things a boy might attempt with a B-B gun that he would not attempt with a slingshot.

The huge pile of refuse, composed of discarded objects ranging in size from a sneaker to a washing machine, was so large that it formed a peninsula of junk that reached out into the deep and dangerous currents. The fast-running water created eddies and whirlpools so strong that when a large wooden crate was tossed in, it would immediately be sucked beneath the roiling surface and then pop up about a hundred yards downstream.

We gingerly stepped around the mountain of throwaways looking for something useful but never took anything back with us. And we invariably encountered foraging river-rats who clearly considered this their territory. They were as big as well-fed cats and unfazed by deftly aimed B-B's or even a marble from our slingshots. As they scurried away, I could swear they looked back and chuckled. We soon gave up our pointless and dangerous forays, largely because of some not-so-veiled threats from the hobos.

I don't advocate that youngsters place themselves in potentially harmful situations, but boys will be boys, and the search for excitement in the real world, instead of in front of a television set, might provide more valuable lessons and a proper respect for real danger.

Because we always were prodded by the desire for adventure, even my bike played an important role. I rarely rode it around the neighborhood for fun. Even a ride down to Bunker Hill Park was more of a chore than a pleasure. With the very steep hills and lack of sidewalks, a quick ride down the street meant a long and dangerous push back up the street. I preferred to run to nearby places and take shortcuts through the woods. But my bike, a 24" Columbia, was valuable for long trips. Often Billy Grover, the brother of Diane, my erstwhile dancing partner, and I would tie our fishing rods to the frames and head out to rural Watertown, sometimes as far as ten miles, in search of good bass fishing. Except for the first mile or two, the territory was more of a gentle roll and, even though our bikes were not three speeds, it was easier going.

We found ponds that may have been part of working farms years before, and more often than not would catch bass or pickerel that had never before been tempted by a Daredevil or Hula Popper (my favorite bass lure). Even when we got "skunked," just the anticipation of catching the granddaddy of all largemouths was enough to make our day. And the exercise that came with miles of pedaling was a bonus we weren't even aware of.

Though we spent a great deal of time wandering hither and yon, the focus of our summer life was Bunker Hill Park (now Schofield Park), which opened in 1953. Park is a misnomer. It was actually a playground, a little less than three acres of dirt and spotty turf. There were four swings, four see-saws, a small set of monkey bars, a slide, and a picnic table under a couple of maples, all of which were located on or near the left field foul territory of a softball diamond. Home plate was a mere two hundred feet from those primary gathering spots. Since we played only hardball on the softball field, and since a hardball carries much further and can pack a greater wallop than a softball, it's not difficult to see why those near the left field line were in harm's way. In fact, many well-hit balls carried over the trees and landed on the hoods of cars traveling down Bunker Hill Avenue, which ran in front of the park. Such poor planning by our city fathers meant the younger kids had to work their playground time around our ball games, which usually took up a couple of hours of most summer mornings.

The danger to those near left field notwithstanding, our ball games were not to be denied simply because baseball, for most youngsters of the era, was not only a game, it was a ritual. It simply had no competition. The NFL had not yet been "invented" by television, and the NBA was only about seven years old, and some teams, like the Rochester Royals and Fort Wayne Pistons, were still operating in smaller markets. The league was waiting for the likes of Wilt Chamberlain and Bill Russell to give it the kind of cachet that would enable it to gain broad-based national attention. Baseball not only had the added power of television, but it also had budding superstars like Mickey Mantle and Willie Mays who were coming into their own, as well as established greats like Ted Williams, Stan Musial, and Jackie Robinson. Now they were all there in our living rooms.

But playing was always more fun than watching. Some of our games took place in the more formal setting of Little League. Making the team was not easy, largely because Waterbury organization was in violation of the official national Little League standards. There were only eight teams in a city of more than one hundred thousand. There were supposed to be many more.

I played for the White Sox. Our uniforms were exact replicas of the big leagues', without a sponsor's name on the back. Mert Connor Stadium was a gem. The perfectly manicured field, the press box, the clubhouse, and the outfield fence, which displayed advertising for local merchants, were all reminiscent of a major league stadium.

The well-constructed bleachers offered a telling comment about parental attitudes at that time. They were usually occupied by friends, but less than a handful of parents attended. No pressure, no obnoxious behavior, no embarrassment. We won some; we lost some. We had fun. The national board that governed adherence to the rules eventually caught up to Waterbury's errant ways, but that turned out to be a non-existent issue that summer.

On August 19, 1955, Waterbury and the entire Naugatuck River Valley were ravaged by a terrible, unexpected, and tragic flash flood as a result of hurricane Diane's twelve-plus inches of rain. Mert Connor Stadium was lost forever to the torrential floodwaters. I was lucky. All I lost was my original birth certificate, which was in the stadium's office files.

Though Little League was fun, the best games took place on summer mornings at the park. We chose up sides, and if we were short a player, we would eliminate the right field position. Any ball hit to right field was treated as a foul ball and therefore a strike. The pitcher didn't try to throw bullets. The aim was to have everybody hit. That's what made it fun. We resolved bad calls and other rulings using nothing stronger than a little lungpower, kept track of the innings and the score by making lines in the dirt, and quit when we felt like it. And we did all this on our own, without any parental involvement.

My love of the game was second only to my most treasured possession at that time—my baseball glove. My parents had given me one for my fifth grade Christmas, but were unaware that the style and technology were beginning to change. My gift was an older four-fingered model glove with a large thumb and too much padding and was already being replaced by a superior product. I quietly decided to buy a new three-finger, hinged model. Because I was involved in the downtown YMCA's swimming program that winter, just a fifteen-cent bus ride away, I was able to search for a new glove. One day, instead of coming home directly after swimming, I raced over to Biener's Sporting Goods, then a few doors down to Alling Rubber Sports Shop. That's when I saw it—the Rawlings ("Finest in the Field") Stan Musial autograph model. It was $9.95, a considerable sum of money then. I wasn't about to ask my parents for help. They had, after all, spent good money for what they thought was a nice glove. Even if they were willing to help after one of my intensive explanations, I wasn't about to hurt their feelings. No parent wants to think he bought a Christmas gift that was not quite right. I prayed for snow that winter. Clearing driveways meant money and that meant a new glove in time for the spring. My prayers were answered. That March I asked my father to take me to Alling Rubber Sporting Goods after work. I couldn't hide the fact that I was buying a more modern glove, so I explained to him that the deep built-in pocket and the hinged style would help me to play better. I told him I had saved enough to buy it, and I think my reasoning had compensated for any hurt feelings. He came in the store to watch me make the biggest purchase of my life and smiled all the way home.

As soon as I was in the door, I meticulously rubbed Neatsfoot Oil into the entire glove, taking care to tenderly massage the fingers, web, and pocket. I positioned a hardball in the pocket and then tightly wrapped the glove around the ball with several feet of cord. The glove's value went way beyond its price simply because I paid for it with my own efforts. The bonus was that my parents were proud of me. They didn't say anything, but as most kids do, I had learned to read their thoughts.

The redolence of the newly oiled leather was intoxicating and gave rise to thoughts of greatness on the field. That wonderful smell stayed with me all that night. No wonder. I had taken the glove to bed and placed it next to my pillow. I drifted off to visions of myself standing in center field, knees bent, glove at the ready, waiting for Allie Reynolds to throw the next pitch.

In retrospect, there was, however, one thing missing on baseball fields at the park and all over this country. Girls. For a variety of reasons, none of them very good, school age girls were not involved in sports. So many girls who had the talent, and, more importantly, the desire to play sports that boys played, had no opportunity. I can't help but think of Waterbury's greatest female athlete, Joan Joyce, who, pitching a softball, struck out Ted Williams twice in a 1961 exhibition game for the Jimmy Fund in Waterbury. She also played on the LPGA Tour and bowled professionally. What is truly regrettable is that her remarkable talent went largely unrecognized because she was born too early. How many other potentially talented girls never reaped the recognition or scholarships that boys did? Happily, the benighted mentality that denied girls the joy of sports then, is now part of the past. For a generation where I see much of legitimate concern, this is truly one of the bright spots.

Every summer, as certain as the crabgrass and clover, comes the bumper stickers warning, "School is out. Watch out for children." I'm not so sure we need them anymore. I live in a neighborhood teeming with children, but the only time I see them is on their daily walks to and from school. In the warm weather it seems as if they have been spirited away, not to be released until school begins again. The baseball fields, the backyards, the playgrounds are empty save for those few activities organized by adults.

One reason I didn't mind going to bed early when I was a kid was that I usually came home exhausted from a hard day's play, right up until my curfew at dusk. When I finally turned in, I was already contemplating the next day's activity.

Like every other stage of life, those moments of outdoor play in our early years, filled with joy, excitement, beauty, and wonderment, are the stuff childhood is made of, and once passed, are gone forever. The child who does not experience life beyond the living room can never go back and gain the learning, exercise, and fun those years should provide. Mom had the right advice, "Go outside and play."

Chapter 25

Hey there toots
Put on your dancin' boots
Come dance with me . . .

Jimmy Van Heusen
Sammy Cahn

Wednesday mornings were the worst during the first few months of fifth grade.   Those were the mornings after, when so many of my classmates and best friends were all aflutter about the doings of the previous evening. They had been enrolled at Miss Reems' Dancing School, and Tuesday nights meant that young ladies and gentlemen from all over town would gather to learn how to dance. In retrospect, I am still amazed by such doings because our crowd was not destined to spend future evenings at debutante balls. I'm not sure how something somewhat pretentious for a ham-and-eggs kind of town got its impetus. Maybe there were more social climbers out there than I had realized. The reasons notwithstanding, I do know that once that engine which feeds on social status gets going, it can be very powerful. What was worse was that I, if only briefly, became caught up in all the silliness that attends such matters. A new, somewhat formal social circle had been formed, and I found myself on the outside looking in. I was, in a word, envious.

No one had excluded me. All it would have taken was a dollar or so each week, a trip to the dancing school to sign up, and I was in. There was, of course, the problem of Norma and Al. I don't remember if I actually approached them with the idea, but I knew they were not about to throw away money to satisfy my yearning to be part of the "in" crowd. So there I sat on Wednesday mornings, in a green-eyed stupor, trying to envision my friends' evenings at dancing school, filled with gaiety and lively chit-chat while they actually learned how to dance.

I knew this was a social skill I had to have. Only a fool could ignore the complete joy I saw on the faces of Fred and Ginger as they tripped the light fantastic (and fantastically) across our television set in a rerun of one of their 1930's classics. A year later, on their TV show, Arthur and Kathryn Murray reinforced my notion that a life without terpsichorean skills was barely worth living. I had even noticed Mom and Dad gracefully floating across the dance floor at a couple of older cousins' weddings. Life had been so easy before this, but now the truth had sunk all the way down to my size 6 ½ triple E bluchers—I did not know how to dance. I was in trouble.

All this fuss and bother was in response to the dances at the Bunker Hill Congregational Church gym. Borrowing from the World War II USO tradition, they were dubbed "canteens"—Friday nights for fifth and sixth grade; Saturdays for seventh and eighth. The price of admission was twenty-five cents, ten cents for a soda, a nickel for a chocolate chip cookie. A record player sat on the floor of the stage and one of the mothers spun those 78's. And I didn't know the foxtrot from the bunny hop, except that both had something to do with animals.

Desperate times call for desperate measures. I had to teach myself. After carefully observing television characters dancing, I took a throw pillow from the couch, went into my parents' bedroom, stood in front of the full length mirror on their closet door, held the pillow against my chest with my right arm, extended my left hand— and froze. I had seen people dance on TV but never watched their feet. I was lost. I had to do the unthinkable.

I turned to Mom who was far more co-operative than I thought she would be. The radio in the kitchen was on, as it always was. She fiddled with the dial until she found music she thought appropriate. I felt uneasy and strange when I had to place one hand on my mother's hip and hold her hand with the other. I giggled. She smiled. "Pay attention," she cautioned. I was awkward and embarrassed, but I didn't have to look her in the eye, I was too busy looking down at our feet. She taught me a simple box step as Nat King Cole crooned "Too Young." "Don't lift your feet, slide them along the floor."

Easy for her to say, but, after a second go-around, I began to get the hang of it.

For the following few weeks I practiced with my pillow until I finally felt I was ready to go to the next Friday night canteen. Around quarter to seven I cut down through the woods and approached the door to the gym where others, all dressed in school clothes, were already gathered. I joined my fellow fifth and sixth graders who chatted about whatever kids that age talk about. I said little. I was a nervous wreck, not so much because of my fear of not being a good dancer, but because I was about to enter a whole new social experience. This wasn't chasing girls around the skating pond and stealing their hats. I had to actually ask a girl to dance, talk to her, and not ruin her shiny patent leather shoes.

The doors opened. Mrs. Hallock took our quarters and stamped the back of our hands. The boys gathered on the left, the girls on the right. Only half the lights were on, so I was able to find a darker spot in a corner. And then Perry Como's soft voice filled the gym. Bill Schofield grabbed me, led me across the gym floor and introduced me to one of the few girls who was shorter than I. I didn't know her because she was from Russell School. I breathed a little easier in the knowledge that if I were going to make a fool of myself, at least it wasn't with someone I would see on a daily basis at Bunker Hill. "Why don't you ask her to dance," he suggested. I swallowed hard; she said yes.

Her name was Marguerite Pomponio and she was a stunning, green-eyed cutie. I think Bill had set up the whole thing, but her warm smile allayed my fears. And it sure wasn't the same as dancing with Mom.

We danced to all the pop tunes of the day. Songstresses with alliterative names were easiest to remember and among the most popular. The vocal stylings of Kitty Kallen, Gogi Grant, Joni James, Kitty Carr, Patti Page, and Doris Day still buzz about in my brain. I wonder if they all had the same agent.

My dancing skills improved, and I became particularly adept at the bunny hop and the Mexican hat dance, but for some reason we never formed a conga line. One method of adding a little spice and mystery was the "shoe" dance. The boys were asked to turn their backs, and each girl would toss one of her shoes into the center of the dance floor. The boys would then turn, go to the pile, select a shoe, and dance with its owner. I was always careful not to select a larger shoe so I wouldn't have to stare at a taller girl's midriff as I danced with her. Nevertheless, it was a fun way to get the kids to mingle a little more. The dance that carried the most social weight was the ladies' choice. It was the boys' turn for the nervous giggles and blushes, and we got a little taste of what so many girls went through in hoping Mr. Special would ask them to dance.

Dances continued to be a big part of our lives through high school. There were "Y" socials on Tuesday nights at the YMCA and on Fridays at the YWCA. There were even dances on Monday nights after CYO (Catholic Youth Organization) meetings in many parishes all over town.

"Good Night, Sweetheart, Good Night" signaled the end of our canteens—9:00 o'clock for the younger kids, 9:30 for the older. It was all great fun, but there were also many subtle benefits. The distant trumpeting of our hormones grew louder every year, but we behaved like gentlemen as we came to see girls as something more than the object of our mindless teasings. Our behavioral changes did not go unnoticed by the girls. There was usually polite conversation and always respect for their person. And no adult ever had to step in and break up a clutch that went beyond the bounds of propriety.

Certainly there is a connection between sexual awakenings and dancing. But what held those mysterious urgings in check and gave us a sense of self-restraint was the society we lived in. We were hardly angels, but we did not grow up in a world drenched in sexual images. Young boys were usually well behind girls in maturing and for the most part controlled their behavior with them, if not their thoughts, because of society's dictates.

Those dictates, especially as kids perceive them, have changed. Today's youngsters have grown up seeing young, barely-dressed celebs bumping and grinding their way across television and movie screens. The message young boys and girls get is clear. But sadly, both are victims. They are thrown into situations that can lead to trouble. I don't think I have to draw pictures. The volatile mixture of what youngsters see, combined with the social pressure to fulfill perceived expectations have become simply too hot for many organizations and school districts to handle. Some school officials are well aware of the potential for trouble and embarrassment and as a result are reluctant to hold dances. One wealthy and sophisticated Connecticut town termed its middle school dances as "fun times," fearing that the term "dance" carried sexual connotations. How could the meaning of something as simple and innocent as a grammar school dance become so twisted? Go figure.

Chapter 26

. . . it was all   Shining,
it was Adam and maiden . . .

Dylan Thomas

I sat at the pond's edge mesmerized by the near hypnotic stitch and whir of the crickets and grasshoppers, summer's last chorus. I warily eyed the sewing needles darting in and out of the nearby cattails, even though I no longer feared that they could sew up my ears. Besides, my mind was on more important matters.

Peggy Schofield and Ernie D'Angelo, the park counselors, had just given the kids a punch-and-cookies party to wrap up Bunker Hill Park's first season. It was the last day of August, 1953. Labor Day was only a week away and school always began on the following Wednesday. The real world kept rolling along: Sir Edmund Hillary had conquered Mt. Everest; the Korean Conflict was over; Lucy's baby had appeared on the first cover of T.V. Guide; and the Yanks were on their way to their fifth consecutive World Series Championship. But my world was changing and becoming more confusing, in some ways more sensed than understood.

As the long, lazy days of August edged toward the beginning of school, something I always looked forward to, I realized I didn't know who was going to be my sixth grade teacher. In years past, on the last day of school, Promotion Day as we called it, we were brought into the classroom of our new teacher. She would make a few brief remarks, the usual looking-forward-to-a-great-year stuff, and, with our final report cards in hand, we would then head for home and all the promises of summer. But on the final day of fifth grade, Miss Fitzgerald told us our new teacher was yet to be named. There was no great consternation over the uncertainty, but I was getting old enough to know that the "wrong" teacher could mean a year of plodding and yawns. Still, the question of who would be my teacher was only a minor consideration.

The confusion that I sensed but could not understand was probably what prompted my moment of solitary contemplation by the pond. What was true in the fifties and, I presume, still is today, was that young boys about to enter the sixth grade were approaching a watershed, a defining moment in their lives. Their hormones were beginning to stir and their social world began to take on a new aura. In short, we were teetering on the edge of puberty. A growing sense of self, coupled with the lingering elements of childhood, can cause more than a little confusion, along with some pretty bizarre behavior.

For these reasons and more, the coming school year was going to be a very different year—a year in which one teacher's evaluation of not only my schoolwork, but also of me as a person, was to make a lasting impression and would, in retrospect, make my year in sixth grade the best and most rewarding of all my years in school before or since.

A pair of water spiders skated by on the pond's still, green water. They seemed to know where they were going. I was not sure where I was headed in life, but the dinner hour was fast approaching, and I knew I had better start up the hill toward home. There were still rules in my life, and one of them was not to be late for dinner.

Chapter 27

*If you press me to say why I loved him, I can say no
more than it was because he was he and I was I.*
Michel Eyquem de Montaigne

I don't think that growing up is a slow, gradual process. Life seems to come at us in bumps and jumps. Though it can be tough to cope with at any particular point, sometimes we get lucky; we step into the light of that one shining moment. Such was my experience in sixth grade, a year made perfect by one man.

The school secretary herded us into our new room as soon as we arrived. We sat there all abuzz with curiosity about who our new teacher would be. We didn't have long to wait.

If I could have frozen the moment, his entrance would have looked something like a Norman Rockwell painting. Everything was there for us to see as he blew into the room and crossed to his desk in the far left corner. A gray Harris tweed jacket, charcoal gray slacks, a blue button-down shirt with a black and yellow rep tie, and spit-polished shell cordovans, all moving at a brisk pace. He turned and gave us a boyish, incandescent, gap-toothed smile that had the enthusiasm, authority, and hint of mischief of a young man on a mission. His name was Jack Delaney.

Though it would be more than a decade before *Star Trek* introduced us to the term "deflector shield," mine was already up. This was the first male teacher I had ever had. Our smart-ass quips and knowing looks were going to be put on hold for a while.

After the pledge and the prayer, in a gravelly voice that sounded as if someone had taken a rasp to his vocal chords, he called out our names and looked each one of us in the eye as we responded. When he called my name and I saw his smile, I lowered my protective shield and knew there would be no need for any derisive words or looks. He was the real deal. He was young, only thirty I learned many years later, street smart, and hip. We shortly learned that he was a Korean War Era vet and a very good athlete. And his good looks didn't hurt. He had everything necessary to garner giggles from the girls and admiration from the boys.

He printed "Mr. Delaney" on the blackboard in a hand less elegant than my past teachers. Then he turned to address the class and gave us a thumbnail sketch of what we would be doing for the rest of the year. He would be our only teacher because our sixth grade classes were then self-contained.

What he couldn't tell us was that his effect on us would go well beyond the boundaries of the curriculum. He treated students in a manner that tended to bring out the best in them. He gained our allegiance, not only with his honesty in evaluating our work, but also with a pat on the shoulder, friendly teasing, or with words of praise for the entire class to hear. He showed many of us who were not top achievers what we were capable of. He believed in us, and we felt compelled not to disappoint him. There is no better kind of motivation for youngsters.

I don't think his teaching techniques were so much planned as they were intuitive and instinctive. Most of the material was familiar stuff. In the language arts portion of the curriculum we wrote and read more. Essay tests were more common as well as written and oral book reports. Math involved more word problems and placed an emphasis on fractions. We would not cover decimals and percentages as well as science until seventh and eighth grades. The apparent thrust of the sixth grade curriculum was strong development of verbal skills and cultural literacy. The latter is that common body of general knowledge and terms that is so lacking in kids today at all levels.

After Delaney reviewed the more familiar material, he pulled a book off the top of what looked like a set of encyclopedias. While I was groaning over the thought of plowing through a book as thick as a two-by-four, he used the term "social studies." I had been introduced to geography in fourth grade and American History in fifth, but I was impressed and curious about this term, which was new to all of us. I don't know when that specific course title entered the jargon of school curricula, but I found it to be that year's most intriguing subject.

Social studies was more than the study of what happened. It was a blend of anthropology, archeology, civics, geography, and history, and maybe even a little sociology. This montage was meant to give us a more complete picture of what came before us, and how the movement and development of Western Civilization, from the Fertile Crescent and Mesopotamia to Greece and Rome, through Western Europe and into England, eventually led to the beginnings of America as a colony and then later as a nation.

Before we began our study of this nearly four thousand-year journey, which stopped just short of the Pilgrim's sail for the New World, we took a great step backward. We went back to the Stone Age and met Peking, Java, Neanderthal, and Cro-Magnon man. As a child I had heard of so-called "cave men," but I had never attached the term to anything other than cartoon images. I began to realize what these ancestors of mine had to do to survive, and how their crude efforts had an underlying sophistication that would lead to the discoveries and inventions that gave us modern society. As Mr. Delaney carefully and repeatedly pointed out, these people were curious about the world around them. It was that curiosity that brought them out of the Stone Age and into the Bronze and Iron Ages; that led them to examine and discover ways to survive and flourish.

Between the sixties and nineties I saw in my own students a sharp decline in that sense of curiosity that had driven us forward. Most students seem to care less and less about the past. Even their parents began to question my course content. Because I was required to teach a great deal of British literature, both the text and I provided considerable historical background. Why was all the history required in an English course, parents wondered. I pointed out that great literature cannot be taught in a vacuum; that the history and literature were inextricably connected. Many just looked back at me with blank faces.

I find now that so many students think history began when they were born. When I explained to my classes that our lives are merely a blink in the march of time, some became upset. "It was like you were telling us there was no Santa Claus," a former student told me a few years later. I pointed out that a look at the past can help society avoid some pitfalls in deciding which steps to take into the future. She felt that only now—the moment—was what counted.

She is probably a parent now. Will she pass on that attitude to her child? Studies indicate that is already the case. And that is why I believe a colleague of mine who taught history spoke for countless teachers when, upon his retirement, he confessed that he felt like a dinosaur in the classroom.

The same material that Delaney taught us is still being taught. Why isn't it being learned? Attitude is the key. If parents don't truly believe certain knowledge is important, neither will their children. And, as an old professor cautioned a young, eager teacher decades ago, "The student that won't be taught, can't be taught."

Fortunately, in 1953, we could be taught. Not only had the society around us made it clear that everything in school was important, but our teachers also reinforced that attitude. That's why Delaney's methods were particularly effective. As he was talking about the material, or indicating key locations on the roll-up maps, he would ask pointed questions of specific students. He handed one of us the pointer and asked for an explanation of who William the Conqueror was, and to please point out to the class where the Normans crossed into England from France and why. At first, the unprepared or unsuspecting student almost had to be revived with smelling salts after Delaney handed him the pointer, but it didn't take us long to catch on. By constantly calling on us, no matter what the subject, we knew that we had to be prepared—*had* to do the homework. If not, we risked humiliation in front of the entire class, not because we didn't know the right answer, but because we didn't try.

I was caught a few times, but the worst was my failure to be prepared for an oral book report. We all knew the day we had to be ready, but we didn't know whom he would call upon. I had read only half of *Tom Sawyer*, so I sat there doing my best to blend into the furniture. Why I thought I could get away with it says something not only about kids at that age, but also about how all of us, at one time or another, so foolishly bet against overwhelming odds.

Lost in thought, I faintly heard a familiar voice call my name from the end of a long, dark tunnel. As I floated back to the moment, I heard it again and knew I was in big trouble. I was going to need more than smelling salts. A defibrillator might have been more in order. Instead of telling the truth, I had the chutzpah to think I could actually fake my way through the telling of a story that I hadn't finished. I started off well enough, but the stall was inevitable. "You didn't read it all, did you Jerry?" He knew; I knew; they all knew. I stood there naked before the class, utterly humiliated. It probably lasted no more than a second before he asked me to be seated. It was unquestionably the longest second of my school career. At the end of the day, Mr. Delaney told me that I would read the remainder of the book and complete my report the next day.

I raced home from school at three-thirty, went into my room, lay on my bed, and began to read the 150 pages I had not finished. I had no idea how I could possibly read all that by the next day. My parents knew I was up against the wall, but stood clear. I spent no more than ten minutes at the dinner table and went back to my room. When my brother came in to go to bed at around eight-thirty, I moved down to the basement and sat on an old glider as I continued to read every word of a story I thoroughly enjoyed. I finished well past my nine o'clock bedtime, but there was no objection from my parents. I went to bed a little less angry with myself, proud because I had finished more than half of a three hundred page book in one night, and comfortable with the thought that I could at least partially redeem my credibility as a good student with Mr. Delaney.

I successfully finished my report before the class the next day, and Mr. Delaney thanked me with a big, warm smile. He was happy I had made good on my promise to finish so much of the book, and I was happy to be back in his good graces.

The pain of that experience has never left me. I had received the best grades of my life from him because I wanted so much to please this man whom I revered. He had shown me what I could do if I worked hard, and I had let him down.

At no point did Mr. Delaney shame me. I had done a pretty good job of that all by myself. Of course, I had grown up in a family, school environment, and society that had no problem with the concept of shame. In fact, and contrary to present day beliefs, shame only temporarily hurts our self-esteem. It encourages us to avoid those dreaded moments by doing the right thing, and by doing so we actually enhance our self-esteem. Less aggravation makes for a happier kid.

What propelled Mr. Delaney into near legendary status was not just his methodology in teaching us about the Crusades or the Renaissance. On recess duty he occasionally joined one of our fifteen-minute touch football games. When he quarterbacked, he demonstrated a powerful and accurate throwing arm. And when he caught a pass, he could outrun us. As one of the faster kids in the school, I found that amazing. He was just out of reach, tie flying over his shoulder and leather-soled cordovans slapping against the asphalt—and I couldn't catch him. How could a man run faster than a kid, I thought. Of course, it never occurred to me that he was a very young man in great shape. Maybe it's because I think kids saw adults with different eyes then. Adult men or women were adults whether they were eighteen, thirty, or fifty. I even regarded a sixteen-year-old baby-sitter as something quite apart from the world of kids. Today, kids see fifty or sixty-year-old rock stars as part of their world. One benefit for those older people in our world was that, because they were not viewed as equals, they had at least a measure of our respect and fear. When, as sixth graders, we attended late summer practice sessions of the sixteen and seventeen-year-olds on Crosby High's football team, we felt that we were in the presence of men. We were intimidated by their walk, their talk, even their sweat. I'm not sure why that line between kid and adult (or should I say perceived adult) has become so blurred today, but in the long run, I don't think it serves either side well.

Not only was Delaney a good athlete, but he also responded to some of our innocent mischief in kind. On a couple of occasions we dared to hurl a snowball in his direction. He always returned our assault with a couple of rockets that scared the hell out of us. We couldn't top him. He was the brains and the boss in the classroom, and the master of the schoolyard.

His punishments for our misbehavior were tough, valuable, and sometimes hilarious. As already noted, sixth graders can be a little braver and more rambunctious than younger students. When the class got a little too itchy, he rarely kept us after. With few exceptions we lived or died as a class. To demonstrate that we were responsible not only to him, but also to each other, he would slap us with a blanket punishment. His favorite was to issue an additional homework assignment. Write the two through twelve times tables ten times each. No carbon copies, thank you. Many modern educators, pseudo-intellects who would cringe at such punishment and point out that we might have grown up with a lasting fear and hatred of the multiplication tables or some other such nonsense, would avoid such a step. And, of course, would also avoid the wrath of parents and school administrators who have been weaned on such pap. They would be very wrong. Most of grammar school math then was centered around computational math—multiplication, division, fractions, decimals, and percentages. Mr. Delaney's "punishment" gave us such complete and near perfect knowledge of the times tables that answering related questions became a matter of reflex, and we could, therefore, solve problems with ease and speed. Ironically, the consequence of our misbehavior served as both a deterrent and a learning tool.

Solid and creative teaching techniques are of primary importance, but the more kids like the teacher, the more valuable those techniques become. What elevated Delaney from the level of very good teacher to icon was his sense of humor. He would find a way to tease each of us and we loved it. Kids like the attention, like to know they are not (thank you Pink Floyd) just "another brick in the wall."

On one occasion Bill Schofield, Rick Lorton, and I got a bit too chatty. Delaney couldn't keep us after school that day because we had a ball game. We were members of the sixth grade baseball team (there was also an eighth grade team) which he coached. That didn't mean we were off the hook. He announced that the three of us would regale the class with a song the next day, or stay after. We agreed to sing, but it would have to be from the back of the classroom. He concurred but added, "We'll see how good you guys really are."

That jibe apparently came from his discovery that the three of us (plus Phil Beach who was in Miss Stone's class) had represented Bunker Hill Park in the annual Barber Shop Quartet Competition the previous summer. The contest took place at the Hamilton Park Pavilion every summer where about fifteen city parks participated. That year, Peggy Schofield, our park counselor, coached us through "Dark Town Strutter's Ball" ("I'll be down to get you in a taxi, honey, better be ready 'bout half past eight"), and "You Must Have Been a Beautiful Baby." The next year our other counselor, Ernie D'Angelo, supplied us with spiffy waiter outfits from his family's restaurant.

We looked great but sounded awful. Trying to get four-part harmony out of four boys whose vocal chords had a mind of their own was impossible. And standing on a stage before a live microphone in front of hundreds of spectators didn't help. The girls' equivalent was the Floro-Dora Competition. They were much better.

Though it was rumored that many parents' eardrums were permanently damaged, the event was always a rousing success because of the spirit in which it was received. All of us tried our best, and the parents were naturally proud of our efforts, but what made the whole thing work was that we weren't preoccupied with being "cool." The participation and the competition on a fairly large scale raised the level of excitement and made it all great fun. (I recently saw a wonderful film entitled *Mad, Hot, Ballroom*, about New York City school youngsters' ballroom dancing competition. The same spirit we experienced prevailed then as well. We need more of this.)

On the assigned day we stood at the rear of the room, thankful that we didn't have to face our classmates. We chose "The Gang That Sang Heart of my Heart." We had memorized it the night before. Our classmates cringed, Delaney smiled, and we learned our lesson, though it wasn't really clear who suffered greater punishment, the singers or the audience.

There were times, however, when Jack Delaney had to do more than issue a friendly edict. Every May the Bunker Hill Congregational Church held a rummage sale in the church gym. For twenty-five cents you could walk away with someone's old toaster or breadbox. And though I am not a bargain hunter, I'll bet an old dress wouldn't have sold for much more.

We had just settled in at our desks, ready for a quiet afternoon session of learning, all the while staring dreamily out the windows on a beautiful May afternoon. We apparently weren't the only ones distracted by spring fever. Delaney rose to begin the class but hadn't uttered two words before he noticed that Jimmy Sullivan and Bill Scavone were missing. Why hadn't they returned from lunch? Someone volunteered that they were last seen at the rummage sale where many of us had gathered before hustling down the avenue for our afternoon class.

As I mentioned earlier, he was a take-charge guy. It was only natural that he chose our classmate, Aldonna Wedge, a take-charge girl, to sit at his desk for what he said would be no more than a ten-minute absence. Her pencil at the ready, Aldonna's look made clear she would follow his directions to the letter. Delaney's command and her glare were enough to guarantee no misbehavior on our part.

He flew out the door. The church gymnasium was only about a three or four minute walk up the street. Delaney probably made it in about a minute. As promised, he returned less than ten minutes later with Jim and Bill in tow. They had apparently lost track of the time and, as they later reported, knew they were in trouble when Mr. D. stormed into the gym. Rather than face him, they tried to hide among the racks of women's dresses. And that is precisely were Delaney found them, along with two lovely gingham prints, which he had under his arm when he returned. He explained that since Bill and Jim were "looking" at dresses, he thought they should have a chance to try them on and model them for us.

A moment later the two most masculine boys in our class returned wearing the dresses, over their regular clothes, thankfully. Both gracefully strode back and forth before the class, and each laughed as hard as we did. The moment worked not only because of Delaney's offbeat sense of humor, but also because the boys had the right attitude. After the fashion show and back in their regular clothing, both returned to the classroom where the laughter had not yet stopped. Finally, we all settled down and got on with the more normal business of the day.

So much more lies in this anecdote than the humor of the situation. Were Mr. Delaney teaching today, none of this would have happened, unless he were willing to face certain disciplinary action and possible dismissal. And given the opportunity, I'm sure he would have thought twice before choosing to leave a class unattended. But I'm equally sure his action was not just an impulsive response. He knew we would behave, and that it was understood that Aldonna, our monitor, had the authority to keep us in line. If we defied her, we were defying him, and none of us would even dare entertain such a notion. I think he went to the church gym rather than report the boys absent knowing it was a quicker and cleaner solution.

Today, in the unlikely event that he survived the first charge, there would be other problems, and, no doubt, parents to contend with. There would be claims that he sought to destroy Jim and Bill's self-esteem with the ersatz fashion show. There might also be claims of sexism woven into the picture based on the political proclivities of the claimant.

The fact remains that it all happened, and nothing detrimental came of it. As expected, we behaved in his absence, Bill and Jim willingly went along with the joke, we all learned that Mr. Delaney was very serious about our being in our seats on time, and everyone had a good laugh.

Delaney had that inimitable gift to mix laughter and caring with the serious business of learning. He was a loving surrogate parent and big brother who became all things to all of us. His praise and punishment kept us moving in the right direction. And he didn't stop caring about us when we left his class, as I was soon to discover. The love and admiration we, his first class, felt continued throughout his career, even when he later moved on to teach at the high school level.

I stayed close to him while at Bunker Hill and often ran into him in all the years that followed. And every time I did, that same special feeling always welled up in my throat, almost to the point of tears, when he gave me a hearty handshake and a hug.

He was, indeed, very special.

Chapter 28

Hold fast the time. Guard it, watch over it, every
hour, every minute!
Unregarded it slips away . . . Hold every moment
sacred.

Thomas Mann

In astronomy the term *syzygy* most often applies when three heavenly bodies line up and cause an eclipse. Or, as was the case a few years ago, when astronomers around the world were particularly excited by the ultimate of such events. All nine planets were positioned in a perfectly straight line, an event that will not occur again for thousands of years. Other than the fact of the rarity of this planetary alignment, I am not sure of its significance.

To a great degree that same questioning might have applied to my own life. I'm not sure of their significance, but I am sure that, in addition to my serendipitous meeting with Jack Delaney, a series of unconnected events lined up to make my sixth grade year even more of a one-time experience. A kiss, the Boy Scouts, and two near disasters, more the stuff of sitcoms than real life, all found a permanent niche in my memory.

The Kiss

I don't think we're ever sure of how such things happen. Did my offhand remark about her blue eyes find its way to her ears? Had she said something to her emissaries who then passed it on to my friends? I do not know. But I do know that one day in the autumn of sixth grade it was somehow decided that Jackie Klies and I had become an "item," in a sixth-grade kind of way.

I remember being overcome by two reactions—incredulity and elation. A born pessimist, I wondered how any member of the opposite sex, especially one with a blonde pixie cut and cornflower blue eyes, could be interested in me. Our house did, after all, have a couple of mirrors, and I knew what I had seen. It wasn't very pretty. But along with the disbelief came that lighter-than-air sensation that usually accompanies such moments. In about two seconds, I went from being part of the moiling crowd to being somebody. Like Charlie Brown, hopelessly smitten by the little red-haired girl, or Rudolph the Red-Nosed Reindeer, captivated by the fluttering eyelashes of the lovely Clarice, I immediately became airborne and floated through the rest of the school day.

As we paired up to leave school that day, I "naturally" stood beside Jackie. We chatted and giggled as we moved through the hallway and down two flights of stairs to the first level. As the pianist of the day pounded out the "Marine Hymn," we turned to our right for the final walk to the front doors of the school, which were always held open by monitors. Between those two doors stood a steel beam about two inches wide. Caught up in the euphoria of the moment and trying to maintain what little composure I had left, I unintentionally recreated a blunder we have all seen countless times in romantic comedies. I walked right smack into the beam that separated the doors, and almost separated my head from my shoulders.

On the verge of blacking out, I faintly heard the gales of laughter and only dimly saw my classmates' pointing fingers since my right eye was already swollen shut. Jackie steadied me as I staggered. She wasn't laughing. Not only was she truly concerned, but I also think she was genuinely flattered by the fact that I had been paying complete attention to her and none whatsoever to where I was walking.

The next day I invited her to Saturday lunch at my house. She accepted. My mother was caught off guard, but was completely cooperative. Jackie's house was just behind the school so it was only a five-minute walk from my door.

Introductions made, I showed her my electric trains as my mother prepared soup and sandwiches. I explained that my dad was working. She noted that her father, a building contractor, often worked Saturdays as well. And my mother smiled that smile that I imagine all mothers do when they see their little boys first express interest in little girls. After lunch, we watched *Red Ryder* while Mom stayed in the kitchen.

Jackie wore a neatly pressed pair of jeans and a plaid flannel shirt, so I assumed she was the outdoor type. I suggested we take a walk, and we found our way to the small patch of woods at the end of my street. I showed her the foundation of the house that was never to be; we talked of Mr. Delaney and social studies—specifically the Romans, as I recall.

In the middle of the path stood a very large half-buried boulder. We sat on top, side-by-side, searching for more conversation on what was a still, perfect autumn afternoon. Surrounded by sunlight filtering through the canopy of turning leaves, for whatever reasons there are that motivate such things, we leaned toward each other, pursed our lips, closed our eyes, and kissed. It lasted only a second or so, but it was my first and I suspect hers, too. Lost for words, we laughed, then regained our composure and headed for home.

After she thanked my mother for lunch, we walked back to her house, still nervously chatting about whatever came into our heads. We acted as if nothing special had happened, but I think we each knew it had.

After that day, we talked at school and skated with the crowd at the Gunlots that winter. There were no more kisses. I think we just wanted to see what it was like.

And then, just as unexpectedly as it all began, Jackie was gone. Her family moved and I never saw her again. But I will never forget that autumn afternoon kiss and the complete and ineffable innocence of that moment.

The Scout

Lord Baden-Powell probably would have been less than pleased with me, and with good reason.

At the beginning of sixth grade, I joined the Boy Scouts of Troop 11 at Bunker Hill Congregational Church largely because it was near my house and most of my friends, Catholic and Protestant, did the same. Most of my other Catholic friends joined Troop 21 at my parish, Blessed Sacrament, which was a long walk away. Though I'm sure Father Kenney, our Pastor, would not have been pleased, my parents didn't see Troop 11 as a religious extension of the Congregational Church, so the choice was mine.

I was eager for this new adventure for a couple of reasons: the carry-over of the military influence from World War II and Korea was still very much alive for my generation, so I quickly found the quasi-military ritual and structure of the scouts very appealing. My primary reason for joining, however, was the lure and lore of the woods. Hiking, camping, and exploring were something I had done with friends, but the scouts would offer guided and more frequent opportunities.

I quickly moved from Tenderfoot to Second Class Scout and began to earn merit badges with my eye on the rank of Scout First Class. Our Patrol Leader, Rusty Harlow, led us on various missions in the woods high above my house; I got to wear my uniform to school during National Boy Scout Week; and I was selected (out of desperation, I think) as an advisor to a Cub Scout Den, which entitled me to wear a distinctive arm braid, a real attention-getter.

In addition to traditional scouting activities, we helped out with community projects. At the end of the Christmas season we collected all of Bunker Hill's Christmas trees and brought them to an open field about a mile up the road at the edge of the woods. On the Twelfth Night (January 6) at around six in the evening, this mountain of trees was set afire. Hundreds of kids and parents attended. Except for a few errant snowballs, all went well and the warmth of the fire was welcomed against the chill of a winter night. Then, as the ashes settled, we walked the mile back down Bunker Hill Avenue to the church gym for an Abbott and Costello comedy, Looney Tunes, hot chocolate and cookies.

There were other projects such as litter and junk collections, but the real value of these activities lay in the sense of community. None of us realized it then, but the need for responsibility to each other quietly found its way into our consciousness, at least for a little while, and hopefully for the future.

Today the suburbs continue to sprawl even further into what were once rural areas, and our neighbors come and go because of job changes or family problems. It's difficult to stay in touch with a central core of community activity. It's no one's fault; it's just a cultural dynamic that we seem powerless to deal with.

On a much smaller and more personal scale, I recall one scouting activity in which some first-year scouts had to learn to cope with a different kind of group dynamic.

Our first overnight weekend at Camp Mattatuck, the regional scouting campsite deep in the woods of Plymouth, Connecticut, was simultaneously miserable, a lot of fun, and a great, if unintended, lesson in how to roll with the punches.

I was all packed and ready that Saturday morning early in November. I had my Boy Scout knife, my Boy Scout canteen, my Boy Scout compass, and my Boy Scout flashlight. I did not, however, have a Boy Scout down-filled sleeping bag. That was not in the family budget. My Boy Scout Manual explained how to prepare a bedroll from blankets. It further noted that, properly done, this would offer adequate warmth and comfort. I would very much like to meet the person who provided that incredibly inaccurate information. Ricky Lorton and I decided we would double up in a pup tent supplied by the troop.

Early November in Connecticut can be a tricky time of year. That year it was cold—cold enough that the frost had already taken hold and the leaden gray skies yielded no warmth. When we arrived at the camp, Rick and I set up our tent and prepared our sleeping quarters. We were situated about fifty yards away from a stone lodge that housed about twenty-five of the older, veteran scouts.

When the day's activities wrapped up and darkness fell, we sat by one of the campfires and ate our hotdogs, hamburgers, and s'mores. Some of the older scouts told us stories about "the man with the hook" who, they alleged, lived nearby in the woods. They also pointed out that the Girl Scouts were encamped on the other side of the pond. If this myth was supposed to get us excited, it had little effect on me. Had there been some kind of encounter, I wouldn't have known what to do. After all, I was still dealing with the thought of my first kiss. The boredom of the silly and pointless stories, the day's strenuous activities, and the absence of television all made it clear that it was time for bed—or should I say bedroll.

Soon after we settled in, I discovered two things: the ground was hard and bone-chilling cold. I was shivering so hard that my teeth began to chatter. At the same time, I realized Rick had a sinus problem. He lay there on his back and quietly wheezed—though not that quietly for someone only two feet away. We lay there for at least a half hour but could not get to sleep. In addition to the wheezing and shivering, we could hear the older scouts in the lodge, whose yelling and uproarious laughter suggested they were having a camping experience a little different from Rick's and mine. We decided to pay them a visit.

We walked in on pillow fights, wrestling—general mayhem. We told someone we were freezing and asked if we could sit in front of the huge fireplace to warm up. "Sure, go ahead," cackled another who had a strange smile on his face. We sat, the fire blazed, and the place grew noticeably quieter. We warily kept an eye on our backs. What we had no way of knowing was that we should have been careful about what was going to happen in front of us.

Without warning there was a muffled boom and then another and another. Suddenly, Rick and I were covered with hot, sticky Campbell's pork and beans from the cans that had been tossed into the fire just as we had walked in. We grabbed the nearest T-shirt or towel, wiped ourselves off and left. We were red-faced, not from the bean bath, but from the howls we could still hear as we slunk back to our tent.

Shortly after we returned to our bedrolls, Rick was out cold and I was on my way, but still hovered in that nether world between sleep and consciousness. And then I thought I heard the pitter-patter of rain. Perfect. Not just a cold November night, but a rainy, cold November night. Suddenly I realized that the rain was falling only on my side. I even thought I heard a couple of snickers. I awakened Rick as I pushed aside the flap to see what was happening. The "rain" was a couple of the older guys peeing on our tent. Now we could add the stench of urine to the wheezing and shivering. We yelled. Unimpressed, they turned and chuckled all the way back to their lodge.

I stayed with the Scouts through seventh grade and though I took it seriously, I saw my friends begin to drift away. What I had approached with eagerness and the best of intentions no longer held the same priority in my life. As my friends' enthusiasm waned and they dropped out, I reluctantly followed. I marched to the beat of their drum and not my own. I allowed myself the immediate comfort of conformity to their will and ignored my own interests. A mistake.

The Daredevil

How many times has each of us looked back on our childhood and shuddered at the crazy risks we may have taken, the seriousness of which would not be fully realized until decades later? Whether or not our actions were intentional, we marvel at how we survived; how we escaped serious injury or worse. Now, that time long past, we laugh that nervous laughter of an innocent who tempted fate and was able to walk away in one piece, if our parents didn't find out.

I suppose some of us are born with a little more of the daredevil in us than others. And with a bit more good luck. It was a gray, chill autumn afternoon brightened only by another day in Mr. Delaney's class. Rick, Phil, and I were on our way home from school. When we arrived at Rick's house at the bottom of "The Stairs," where Valentine Street met the lower portion of Circuit Avenue, we paused to consider what we could do for the remainder of that afternoon. Not much, we concluded, on this gloomy day with darkness closing fast.

We climbed the first flight of steps and instead of turning to Rick's house on our right, walked to a set of swings in Steele's backyard on our left. As we sat on the swings and chatted aimlessly in the dead quiet of that late November afternoon, strange sounds from high up on the stairs caught our attention. *Thumpa, thumpa, thumpa, grunt—thumpa, thumpa, thumpa, grunt.* The rhythmic beat grew louder as it neared. From our position we could see only about ten feet of the asphalt sidewalk that led to the last flight of stairs.

Sometimes our eyes see what our brain refuses to believe. Still, there was no doubt. Someone had just flown by on a bicycle—a death-defying ride that had apparently begun at the top of the stairs, some four hundred feet and three flights further up. Momentarily frozen by the ugly sound of the crash, we hopped off the swings and ran to the stairs to discover Billy Grover and what was left of his bike at the bottom of the last step. He was conscious but bleeding. The front wheel of his bike and the fork that held it were mangled. Rick's mom called for an ambulance. We helped Billy get up, but he was clearly dazed and hurting. Soon the ambulance came and he was off to the emergency room. We knew Bill was a tough kid, but this stunt had gone a step too far.

Thankfully, Bill turned out to be okay. He was back in our classroom a few days later, the cuts and bruises covered by tape and gauze. He claimed the brakes on his bike had failed, but the police tested them and said they were functioning. Bill told me that his father was furious when notified the brakes worked. He was lucky on two counts. The fall didn't seriously hurt him, and his father, a man who looked as if he could bend rails with his bare hands, withheld his anger. Everyone's attitude was pretty much the same: Bill was okay, thank God.

It was a windy March day, a good day for kite flying, but not at the intersection of Valentine Street and Circuit Avenue near the bottom of "The Stairs." The power lines made it dangerous, not to mention the occasional passing car rounding the steep curve at the bottom of Circuit Avenue. The elderly driver never saw him, and Billy never saw the car since he was moving backward in the middle of the street trying to help his kite gain some altitude.

The red and white Cadillac ambulance once again paid a visit to the same place it had been a few months earlier. Billy was back in school a few days later. He was bumped and bruised but not seriously injured because the car had swerved at the last second and struck only a glancing blow. Bill was going to be okay again, thank God.

It was a beautiful day late in May, as I recall. We had just settled in for the afternoon session in Mr. Delaney's classroom. Billy sat about four seats behind me in the row to my left. We still had the old-fashioned wooden desks with the top that lifted up. Billy's desktop was still up as class began. I was curious about what he was up to, but caught only occasional glimpses of his crew cut.

And then, with no warning, there was a bright flash and a *WHOOMP*. Billy had apparently pulled apart some bullets he had found and accidentally set off a small pile of gunpowder that he was toying with inside his desk. Mr. Delaney sprinted toward the rear of the class as a small mushroom cloud rose above Bill's head. Then up came his charred face, eyelashes, eyebrows, and crew cut, all singed. He looked at once both stunned and otherworldly.

He was quickly taken to the front of the building. The ambulance driver didn't have to go up Valentine Street this time. Bill was off to the emergency room at Waterbury Hospital—again.

He returned a couple of days later, a little the worse for wear, his burns gauzed and salved. He seemed to really appreciate our cheers, which quickly broke into laughter. Bill laughed as hard as we did. He was okay—again. Thank God.

Bad Humor Men

"And what is so rare as a day in June," penned poet James Russell Lowell. And one June day went even a step beyond that. It certainly was perfect weather around one o'clock on that June afternoon in 1954 as our year in sixth grade neared an end. We had just returned to the schoolyard from lunch and were awaiting the bell for the beginning of the afternoon session. In a long-standing tradition at the school, the "big kids," seventh and eighth graders, gathered behind the school on a large play area. The rest of us milled around near the front of the building on Bunker Hill Avenue, the girls on the right side and the boys on the left. Some of the boys bounced a pink high bouncer off the side of the school while a few flipped baseball cards. Others gathered under the shade of a magnificent elm where the sidewalk met the asphalt of the schoolyard. And that's where it began. It wasn't one of those events that altered and illuminated our times—but we were there, to witness and take part in it, and none of us will ever forget it.

Some thirty or forty boys had gathered by the sidewalk to await the Good Humor man, whose arrival was always announced by the distinctive and wonderful sound of those jingling bells. On time as always, he pulled up alongside the curb just in front of us. But this time a new ice cream vendor pulled up twenty feet behind him. This interloper, who dared cross swords with the Good Humor man, was an independent, an entrepreneur in a pick-up truck with what apparently was a huge ice box on the back, covered by what looked like a white, plywood wedding cake with a scalloped top, which sat beneath a small gold dome. All this gave the truck a respectable look, but it didn't have the bells, that distinctive blue lettering, or that clean, white, custom-made truck body with its open cockpit and leather seats. The new fellow's advertising was apparently limited to the hand-painted red brush strokes on the sides of the plywood, which boldly announced CAPITOL BAR. This was a no-frills kind of guy who was ready to do whatever was necessary to sell his ice cream.

The growing crowd gravitated toward the Good Humor truck. Here was a known name, a known product, and a guy in a spiffy white uniform, which had such a strong military presence that I wanted to salute him. The other fellow wore a pair of jeans and a T-shirt and looked a little rough around the edges. In fact, his hairy, muscular arms looked as if they could hoist that icebox on the back of his truck with little effort.

Our dimes were ready for the ice cream sandwiches, creamsicles, small sundaes in a cup, and, the very best of all, toasted almond bars. A few of my impatient classmates with less discriminating taste had drifted over to Capitol Bar's truck, but Mr. Bluejeans knew he was losing this battle to that *faux* naval officer only twenty feet away.

Mr. Capitol Bar, already a penny cheaper on similar items, announced in a stage voice that all ice cream would be eight cents. The crowd immediately shifted to the left. In less than a heartbeat the naval officer proclaimed that all of his bars would go for seven cents. The crowd moved to the right.

The bidding war had begun. What each was selling didn't matter. It had become a matter of price, and Capitol Bar's product turned out to be as tasty as Good Humor's. "Six cents," responded Mr. Bluejeans. No sooner had we taken a step to the left when the ensign, his bowtie beginning to twitch, cried out, "Five cents." The sweat on his brow was from more than the June heat. I think he was beginning to realize that he didn't have the authority to dictate Good Humor's prices; that once he had crossed the line, there was no turning back. That bridge was in flames and he was melting faster than one of his ice-cream bars.

Mr. Capitol Bar, the young entrepreneur, knew about capitalist principles: undercut the competition and you get the business. Of course, there can be a point of diminishing returns. Whether he realized that or just didn't care I'll never know, but he was about to become the ultimate competitor. He reached into the freezer with both hands and came out with a carton wrapped in white paper with no top or bottom. And then those hairy, muscular arms heaved it high into the air, and like all those bigger-than-life moments, everything went into slow motion. An eerie silence blanketed the crowd and, like the last out pop fly of the World Series, all of our eyes were riveted to that package. And then small packets began to fly out of it as the wrapper came loose.

Ohmigod! It was as if a geyser of ice cream bars had erupted from Mr. Capitol Bar's hands, at least two dozen of them, and they were headed for us. This was the stuff a kid's dreams are made of. Then, we jumped back into real time and that handsome, young naval officer with the change maker on his belt let loose with a creamsicle barrage of his own.

The moment was simply too wonderful for us to grasp, for about half a second, then began a mad scramble to grab whatever we could as the rock-hard bars continued to rain down all about us, but no one had to move very far. The two vendors, now gone berserk, continued to heave dozens of bars. There was ice cream everywhere! We stuffed them anywhere we could; in our pockets and even in our shirts, ignoring the freezing cold against our skin.

And then, almost as quickly as it had begun, it was over. They were out of ice cream and we were out of breath. The late bell rang, and being better conditioned than Pavlov's pups, we headed for our classrooms, knowing that to be tardy was to be dead.

Once back in class, we slipped into our seats and stuffed our prizes into our desks. Mr. Delaney, who had been in the teachers' room, walked in a minute later and immediately sensed something was amiss. We couldn't be that excited about his pending lesson on fractions. We quickly settled down and class began, but within a few minutes Mr. D. noticed a white, creamy liquid dripping from the bottom of Toby Nardella's desk. Our wooden desks were as old as the school itself—some had cracked bottoms, some didn't. Either way, we were in big trouble. As Delaney walked over to see what the hell was going on with Toby's desk, I opened the top of mine for a peek. The warm June air had created a small vanilla lake, dotted with tiny islands of toasted almond. Of course, all my books sat in the middle of this mess.

It took a few moments for Delaney to connect the earlier noise from in front of the school and our anxiousness at the start of the class with the melting ice cream in our desks. We immediately told him what had happened. Class was delayed for about forty-five minutes so we could clean out our desks. The girls laughed but kindly helped us. Mr. Delaney announced that those of us who had caused the problem would stay after, but he couldn't wipe the smile from his face for the rest of the afternoon.

As we left school later that day, never having savored our free ice cream, the only thing we could talk about all the way home was the unlikely war we had witnessed. I told my parents, but I doubt that my simplistic description captured the riotous glee of the moment. They laughed and we went on with our dinner.

In reflecting on one of the most unreal moments in my life, two thoughts come to mind: As that afternoon's events unfolded, I remember seeing each vendor's face as the situation built to a fevered pitch. At the height of the battle, for just a few fleeting seconds, I could see that this was no good-natured lark, no crazy, carefree moment. Each of them snarled with a wild-eyed look that bore a deadly and earnest seriousness. I saw something in the behavior of these people that was both bewildering and frightening. These were, after all, adults. I thought nutty behavior, Lucy *et al* notwithstanding, was our bailiwick, a proprietary right of kids. But this wasn't crazy Uncle Charlie pulling our legs out from beneath us in the surf at the beach. Instead, I was reminded of something we had read about in social studies. During that snippet of time, that thin veneer of civilization had been stripped away. The only thing these guys were missing was the bearskin draped over their shoulders and a stone axe. They were, if only for the blink of an eye, out of control and had reverted to a darker, more primitive impulse that wasn't very pretty. It was the same as what I saw when two kids went at it in the schoolyard. Win, lose, or draw, I have never liked seeing it in others, even less in myself, and least of all in adults. I have always been overly sensitive to such moments. I don't know why. And, when all was said and done, I'll bet the bad humor men laughed about it—I hope.

In terms of today's society, I would wager my pension check that there would be a far different result to all this commotion. Back then, both were told they could no longer sell ice cream in front of the school and were required to move a short distance up the street. I'm sure the Good Humor man was either fired or received a severe tongue-lashing from his superiors. I'm also equally sure Mr. Capitol Bar was not about to throw away all his profits again.

Today the event would probably call for a major meeting of school administrators. Boards of education would dictate new policies. PTA's would call for investigations. Parents would be assured that their children's lives would not be jeopardized by flying ice cream bars. And, when the media caught wind of it, serious-faced local anchors would bombard us with in-depth coverage and interviews as well as a sidebar for their "fear-du-jour" segment that would run along the lines of, "Ice cream vendors—friend or foe?"

At any rate, there is no question in my mind that the fallout would be worse than the event. And that raises the question: Wouldn't it be better to adopt a no harm-no foul attitude about issues that really have little or no impact on our welfare? Wouldn't it be better for society's blood pressure to let some things just quietly pass?

And, for the record, toasted almond bars are still the best.

Chapter 29

Some are bewilder'd in the maze of schools.

Alexander Pope

Though there are some significant differences, I think many of us tend to lump seventh and eighth grade together. For those who attended a junior high way back when, that would be an automatic reaction. In my corner of the world, however, there were very few junior highs; in fact, I knew of only one, which opened in a small neighboring town at about the same time I entered seventh grade.

As a youngster, I often read about or saw kids on television in junior high settings. The concept held more than a little appeal for me at that point in my life. It had the ring of "almost" high school, and that offered special status. I would no longer be part of a grammar school. It was a step toward the big time.

During the fifties and sixties some school districts in America already had junior highs; the rest had K-8s. Then, in the seventies and eighties, as is so often the case in education, everyone jumped on the bandwagon and created junior highs, most of which were soon to evolve into middle schools, which also included sixth grades. Once these kinds of juggernauts gain some impetus, those who oppose them are viewed as reactionaries, and those from within the system of a similar voice may well be placing their jobs in jeopardy. But as some teachers and administrators knew well before these decisions, the timing could not have been worse.

Just as the lives of American children were becoming more problematic, youngsters who were already approaching one of the most difficult stages in their lives, even under the best conditions, were thrown together with no buffer. On the other hand, going through seventh and eighth grades surrounded by the same kids with whom we had spent our first six years meant not having to be anything other than what we were—no masks to wear, no new and often silly standards to conform to. If we needed an ego boost, we could be consoled in that we were at the top of the heap in the school. Recently some school districts have realized this and consequently have moved back to or are contemplating a return to the kindergarten through eighth grade school concept.

At first glance, the reasons for the shift to junior highs or middle schools seem perfectly logical. It eases the busing situation, simplifies construction requirements, and allows all the teachers in the school to meet and plan a common curriculum, to mention just a few. The whole concept seems so economical, practical, and logical. So did the dirigible.

But somewhere along the way, amid all the hurly-burly, we forgot the students and their needs, as well as their vulnerabilities. Seventh and eighth grade mark the beginning of a major step in the socialization process and all the pressures and problems that come with it. That point in the lives of today's youth has become every bit as difficult as the first two years of high school were for my generation. Over the last few decades drinking, drugs, sex, and an "attitude" have moved down to the middle school level in a big way. Consider the plight of a young boy or girl just out of fifth grade being thrust into this kind of social dynamic. The demand for conformity—what to wear, what to say, how to behave—can be overwhelming.

In addition to social competition, a child's chance of making the team (or the band, or cheerleading squad) is severely limited in a huge middle school. Several K-8s, instead, would offer several teams and obviously more chances for a student to participate. I might also add that at a stage when being "cool" is of the utmost importance, in a K-8 it's not easy to be impressed with yourself as you're delivering a message to the office and a third grader walks by to remind you of your place in the world, just another part of the buffer I noted earlier. I'm hardly alone in these thoughts. Some large school districts in America have already returned to the K-8 concept. Even the middle-sized town I live in is contemplating a move back.

Those who know and deal with children on a daily basis now realize, especially after having learned some hard lessons, that K-8s keep youngsters a little more innocent a little longer. Those feeding frenzies that their young egos relish, which can be so destructive, are postponed at least for a bit longer. Kids have more time to stay grounded before they have to face the pressures of high school. And that's a good thing.

Chapter 30

The measure of the man is how he runs the last mile.
Anon.

My seventh and eighth grade years can best be described as manic: they truly were years of high highs and low lows. With a few notable exceptions, my memory tends to weave my last two years at Bunker Hill into one tapestry of threads both bright and dark. No doubt the similarity of the course work and the fact that three of my four subject teachers were the same for both years contributed to this sense of sameness. Our socialization process also reinforced the homogeneity of seventh and eighth grade. We gathered together in the schoolyard, segregating ourselves from the younger kids, and we had our own canteen dances on Saturday nights at the gym of Bunker Hill Congregational Church. Physical maturation and sexual awareness, a bit more evident in the girls, accounted for yet another part of the division between seventh and eighth grade and the rest of the school. Nature was not to be denied. We were growing up.

The Teachers

The first problem I had in seventh grade was inevitable—all of my teachers walked in the shadow of Jack Delaney. The Jiminy Cricket in me didn't have to tell me to get my act together and deal with matters at hand. But Delaney's exuberance and vitality just wasn't going to be matched by the five teachers I had to face in my last two years.

Miss Fitzgerald, whom I had in fifth and would have again for history in eighth grade, brought the same uninspiring style to seventh grade English that she had generated in my fifth grade year. She dutifully covered the material, but she was less enthusiastic about being there than we were.

Just as Miss Fitzgerald brought predictability to her classes, John Nolan, my seventh grade history teacher, brought an unpredictability to his teaching that was a source of great amusement, except to those who were his intended targets. He was a good man, a better than average teacher, but he had a tendency to let his temper overrule his good sense on occasion. When he was working at the blackboard and heard someone fooling around behind him (invariably one of the boys), he would, with whatever was in his hand, usually a piece of chalk or an eraser, in one continuous and smooth motion, spin and fling it directly at the student. On one occasion we were singing from a songbook (I can't remember why) and Ralph Fabiano, who unfortunately had a front-row seat, was, in Mr. Nolan's estimation, being less than co-operative. Ralph must have really struck a nerve because Mr. Nolan frisbied the fortunately small and slim songbook at Ralph's head. Ralph, who had already developed a cat-like quickness from past experience, calmly deflected the missile with one hand. No fools we, fear and good instincts told us to just continue singing. Nolan retrieved the book and class rolled on. Between warm-up pitches, Nolan used stentorian pronouncements and dramatic readings of historic poetry to get our attention. It worked. A few years later, however, Mr. Nolan's throwing arm apparently lost its resilience and he moved on to administration.

Forty years later we invited him to our reunion. With his enthusiastic reading of "O Captain! My Captain!" still fresh in our memories, at our request he once again regaled us with a reading of the Whitman classic, although a few of us still flinched as he read. His robust handshakes indicated that his arm remained in good shape. And, at least some of us were still appreciative of how he had helped to develop our reflexes.

One of the academic highlights of my last two years belongs to math teacher Frank Finnan. The math curriculum in our school system called for the study of decimals in seventh grade and percentages in eighth. Both involved the extensive use of word problems and reviewed past material such as fractions. Though none of this is regarded as higher math, some kids struggled with it, and

I'm sure some never got it. Neither of those results could be laid at the feet of Mr. Finnan. His great sense of humor and relaxed manner eased the anxiousness of those who feared math more than the wrath of God. My experience and observations, both as a student and teacher, tell me that though there are many math teachers out there, few have the gift, that uncanny ability to make clear the concepts, the workings of the formulas, and the methods for solving the problems. Whether it be in grammar school, high school, or college, all of us, except for the chosen few, were destined to run into that wall, that state of complete and perfect incomprehension. I sparred with math anxiety when I reached trigonometry, and by the time I was introduced to calculus, I was out for the count. Had I more of the likes of Frank Finnan (or Elizabeth Paul in high school), I might have suffered a less severe bruising.

In order to be a great or even very good teacher, one has to be able to read a student's mind, has to be able to see the problem as the student sees it, whether it's solving a math problem or writing an essay. The teacher then must be able to go into the student's head and clear that fog that sometimes envelops his brain. Nowhere in teaching is the job more difficult than for a math teacher. Most of mine assumed that because they understood it, the rest of us would. That is a mistake that no teacher of any subject should make. But even with that raised level of consciousness, I still believe that it takes an ineffable gift. Mr. Finnan had it.

Mr. Finnan's equally gifted colleague, Mr. Melchionna, my seventh and eighth grade science teacher, had another kind of gift. He made science exciting, which, according to my friends who have taught it, is very difficult today. There is no single reason, but showing kids that the blackboard eraser and a five pound rock fall at the same rate of speed isn't going to draw oohs and aahs from students who have seen countless hours of spectacular special effects and who use technology that my generation saw only in Dick Tracy's wrist radio.

Children's curiosity has also been stultified by a here-and-now society. The prevailing attitude I have seen indicates little care about the fundamental scientific principles behind the technological creation. The attitude is: What can this thing do for me now? Exploration, when youngsters still are naturally curious, is not encouraged. The schools are now too busy teaching kids how to take state and federally mandated tests, and hours spent with Play Station or in front of a television set don't help. Neither do parents who are far more interested in entertainment that gives them insights into every excruciating detail of celebrity life. As kids, we watched prime-time Disney specials about the natural world. That just wouldn't fly today. With my own children, the *Nature* series on PBS was regular TV fare. How many children are given that opportunity today?

Mr. Melchionna had a ready-made audience. We touched on everything from astronomy and physics, to chemistry and geology. It was easy to see he was excited about the subject matter. He moved about the classroom with the energy and alacrity of a well-trained athlete. Along with our crude experiments, we were allowed to bring materials (e.g., unusual rocks, model airplanes) into the classroom and either ask or explain what scientific principles applied to them.

One of the most important educational legacies he gave us went right to the heart of scientific thought. The homework assignment for one evening was to write a paper about what we thought was man's most important invention. Some offered the likes of electric current, the automobile, or radio/television. I believe I chose the telephone. One scholar chose the ambulance.

He collected all of our papers and, without even looking at them, announced that none of us had the right answer. "The greatest invention," he proclaimed, "is the Scientific Method." He smiled at our blank faces, and went on to explain that by taking a step-by-step approach, man has made fascinating and important discoveries. Melchionna wanted us to know that there was a systematic and logical way to discover facts. By observing natural occurrences (e.g., Newton's apple), forming a hypothesis, and conducting experiments, we can arrive at a fact, a truth. The logic of such an approach made sense even to my young mind. That lesson and its importance have never left me.

That pure reasoning, free of emotion, applies not only to physics and chemistry. Much of our children's social behavior and learning patterns can be examined in the same light. When we treat children in a particular manner, we generally know how they will respond. Yet in spite of all the evidence, we continue to raise our children in ways that we know will not bring about desired behavior. We try endless social experiments, throw oodles of dollars at problems that have little or nothing to do with money, and propagate whopping lies to convince ourselves that everything will turn out all right—that our country will not suffer from parenting standards that defy all logic.

I wonder what Mr. Melchionna would say

*****

I continued to slog my way through seventh grade with what can best be described as an uneven performance which improved somewhat as the year went on. Armed with renewed confidence and motivation, I had higher expectations for eighth grade. And with three of my teachers that was indeed the case.

The Dodgers would finally win a World Series in that fall of 1955, and I sensed I was going to have a pretty good year myself. Going three for four is a good day at the plate. Not so good in school. I was getting older and the distant beat of that drummer Mr. Thoreau spoke of was steadily growing louder as I matured. What I didn't realize was that there are occasions when academic self-preservation takes precedence over getting into a debate with one's teacher.

I was eight years old and had first met Mrs. Sutton when she invited my brother and me to watch Howdy Doody in her family room. She lived across the street from our new home, which did not have a television set. Now, five years later, she stood in front of my eighth grade English class. Neighbors or not, from past experience I knew her no-nonsense attitude would not give me any kind of an edge over my classmates. Mrs. Sutton brought a strictly business mien and anxious nervousness to the class. Neither works well, especially with older children. Her presence mixed with the thrills of endless grammar lessons made our daily ritual more of a grind than anything else.

At that point in my life I had pretty much trained myself to cope with whatever kind of teacher fate dealt me. I had also resigned myself to the fact that some material couldn't be made exciting even if Soupy Sales presented it. What kept me afloat was the belief that it was necessary to learn what was being taught. That's where my problem with Mrs. Sutton began.

As one who has spent most of his life teaching English, I clearly understand that students should have at least a reasonable understanding of the grammar of their language. My problem lies with the mistaken notion that endless grammatical drills will somehow make students better writers. In my eighth grade English class we spent months learning the parts of speech, defining phrases, clauses, and the types of sentences, in addition to struggling with the hated verbals (gerunds, infinitives, and participles). Much of this is learned through rote memory. In order to make the whole montage clearer and to help us parse sentences with a more visual approach, we began to diagram them. Mrs. Sutton insisted that we learn to diagram so that we could more easily pull sentences apart and see how all the pieces played a specific role.

Some see this method as valuable—a great teaching tool. In fact, in my early teaching days, our English department required us to teach diagramming. But like those in my college calculus class who could see the unfolding logic of a complex problem, while I grinded my way to a solid F, in my eighth grade English class I was able to see how sentences were strung together. I could "see" the parts of speech, the phrases, the clauses. I take no credit for this. It was as effortless for me as it is for those who pick up a guitar and, at first attempt, can plunk out a tune. Consequently, I made less than a half-hearted attempt to learn diagramming. In my eighth-grade mind I knew that I could pass any test Mrs. Sutton would present. Unfortunately, Mrs. Sutton didn't see the issue as I did. I even had the temerity to ask her if I had to learn to diagram since I could already do what it was intended to teach. She seemed puzzled that I would even ask such a question. Of course, her answer was yes, I had to learn it; it was important. Though I couldn't articulate then what I could later in life, what I was saying was: if diagramming were a means to an end, and I could reach that end without its help, wouldn't I still be accomplishing her final goal? I foolishly dug in my heels, and I lost. I got consistent C's in the grammar portion of the course. Another lesson learned the hard way.

I suspect much of the luckiest generation spent a disproportionate amount of time on lessons that were thought to be invaluable at that point in a student's life. A little over a decade later my department head brought to my attention a study which indicated that older students (high school juniors and seniors) are able to learn grammar much faster than younger students, and that younger students should spend far more time writing and reading the kinds of prose that will help them, regardless of what they choose to study later in life.

Taken as a whole, I had a good learning experience in grammar school. All of my teachers tried to do their jobs. Some succeeded better than others. Later, in high school and college, I had some who didn't even try. Later yet, I learned that teaching alongside those who were incompetent was even more painful because I knew what they weren't doing. Unfortunately, bad teachers will always be a problem. America requires three million teachers to educate its young. That number alone suggests that not all will be good, let alone great. The best way to deal with that problem is to make clear that dealing with all kinds of teachers is the child's responsibility.

My wife and I both taught in the town where our children attended school. Our situation was even more difficult than that of the average parent because we really knew who were the best and worst teachers. When our boys made negative remarks about a teacher, we did what our parents did with us. Collaborative parents only make the situation that much more difficult. "You just do your job," my parents said. That's all. No heart-to-heart talks. No visible signs of sympathy. And that is pretty much as it has to be in the real world. And isn't that what we are supposed to be preparing our kids for?

*****

Outside of the classroom itself, my seventh and eighth grade years brought a personal loss, a natural disaster, one close call, and two especially thoughtful gestures, all of which left lifelong impressions on my mind and heart.

Loss and Disaster

It was early on a cold November evening when next-door neighbor Judy Kelsey, Joan's younger sister, found me on the dance floor at the Saturday night canteen. I could barely hear her words above Kitty Kallen's singing "Little Things Mean a Lot," but the urgent look on Judy's face told me that I had better stop dancing and slip over to a corner to talk to her. She hesitantly told me that our cat, Coco, had been hit by a car and I had better get home. Leaving my jacket behind, I sprinted into the cold night air and raced up the hill. When I burst in the front door, my brother's tears and the look on my father's face were all I needed to realize that she was gone.

Coco was an apparent stray that I had met at the top of "The Stairs" one afternoon in fourth grade. With my encouragement, she followed me home. I spent almost half an hour petting her and, with some small pieces of veal cutlet hidden in my pocket after that night's dinner, I was able to entice her to remain in our backyard. About an hour later, I told my parents that I saw a strange cat near the back door. We were truly a family of animal lovers. Any animal—dog, cat, squirrel, or injured bird—was welcome at our house. As soon as my father found her, she became part of our family. She was a shorthaired tiger with a white spot on her chest. I named her and from that night on she was always at the foot of my bed.

About a year later she bore a litter of four kittens in a blanketed box next to our furnace in the basement. One was stillborn, but the others, two angoras and a tiger-striped shorthair, seemed fine. Shortly after their birth, Coco began an evening ritual that I thought was particularly touching. After they were done nursing, she would take each kitten in her mouth and bring it upstairs to our dining area. She obviously wanted to be with us, and seemed anxious to show off her new brood. As the kittens grew and became friskier, they followed her upstairs and, every evening, around the same time that *Kukla, Fran, and Ollie* aired, all hell would break loose as they frolicked and explored, skidding across the linoleum in the darkened kitchen. Their mother would try to keep an eye on all of them at once, a difficult task for any parent.

These moments, among the very best of my childhood, revealed a warmth and loving touch I had not often seen in my mother. Coco didn't know it, but she provided a focus for our family and created a bond that I had not sensed before.

Now my father, brother Al, and I sat there, speechless, numbed, and teary-eyed. My mother had taken the two-hour train ride that morning to do some shopping with my aunts in New York City. Already exhausted when she knocked on the front door, my father asked us to give her a chance to settle down before we broke the bad news. Dad opened the door. Mom, her arms filled with bags, didn't even make it across the threshold before my brother and I cried out, "Coco is dead!" She gasped, dropped her packages, and sobbed uncontrollably. It was one of the few times I had seen her cry. After years of seeing more of her temper and frustration than anything else, I saw a tenderness and vulnerability that mirrored a humanity which I had not witnessed before. She felt as deeply about my furry friend as I did. I went to bed that night wrapped in inconsolable grief. That warm spot at the foot of my bed would no longer be there. But as time went on, I developed a stronger relationship and a new warm spot for my mom.

*****

It was the evening of August 18, 1955. Noted actress and native Waterburian Rosalind Russell and her co-star Gloria DeHaven were in town for the premiere of their movie *Girl Rush*. In a driving rain at the entrance of the State Theater, Mayor Raymond Snyder revealed a plaque honoring Miss Russell. The movie went largely unnoticed, as would the event itself had it not become inextricably tied to a natural disaster of huge proportions that was only hours away.

Many knew we were in trouble. We had had heavy rain a few days earlier and now the aftermath of hurricane Diane had dumped more than twelve inches of rain in the last twenty-four hours. My Uncle Jim, who lived nearby and was a major in the Army Reserves, called my father at three that morning to tell him that the Thomaston Dam had given way and a terrific flash flood had already begun.

At first light, my father and I jumped into the green beetle and headed down the hills toward the intersection of Bunker Hill and Watertown Avenues. But that morning there was no Watertown Avenue. In fact, the water had crept a hundred yards up Bunker Hill Avenue. What I saw was not a river which usually flowed about fifteen feet below street level, but an ugly brown lake that stretched as far as the eye could see. There were freight cars floating in the current; even a couple of houses quietly glided by. None of it was real. A crowd had gathered at our vantage point, but there was only an eerie silence. This was not a television screen we were watching. None of us had ever seen the raw power of nature firsthand. Before this, the worst I had ever experienced was a bad snowstorm. This tragedy was in another category altogether.

By that afternoon, the water level had dropped by half. But even so, tons of debris and brand new 1955 Buicks, apparently from a dealer's parking lot which had been at the water's edge, continued to float downstream. Everything was coated with mud, which was already drying out in the warm August sun. We were now able to stand on the sidewalk along Watertown Avenue, but the river, normally twenty feet below this point, now flowed only a foot below us. I naively wondered what had become of our beloved Tower Theater a quarter of a mile down the street. Ricky and I had spent countless Saturday matinees watching the likes of *The Steel Helmet*, *The Thing*, and *Rebel Without a Cause*. But the show before us was nothing like what we had seen on the silver screen those many

Saturday afternoons. When the movies were over, we always walked home along the sidewalk situated high above the river.

Within a few hours of what I had witnessed earlier that morning, the casualty reports began to come in. People caught unaware had died—lots of people. And a little of my youthful bravado died with them. For the very first time I realized how vulnerable we are, and that the powers of nature can sometimes render us helpless. I had seen natural disasters on television. But that was there, not here; it happened to them, but it couldn't happen to us. I didn't have that thought so often after August 19, 1955.

A Driving Lesson

As kids I suppose we all had the makings of at least one hare-brained scheme in us. And most of us were probably smart enough or fearful enough not to follow that impulse. In at least one instance, I cannot claim to have been wise or prudent in my response to a temptation that could have had disastrous results. Strangely enough, the upshot of what was clearly a punishable offense led to a further strengthening of the bond with my mother, one that was beginning to improve but still stood on shaky ground.

From the very first moment that my father had let me shift his old Plymouth, I was fascinated with cars. America was fast becoming a car culture, and every year I awaited the unveiling of the new models. I was captivated by innovations such as the wrap-around windshields and automatic transmissions, power steering and brakes. As the engines grew bigger and more powerful, my lust for the open road followed.

Unfortunately, I would see none of these automotive improvements until we acquired a used 1954 Buick Special in 1957. Dad always bought used cars. His frugality was supported by the fact that my mother didn't drive and his annual mileage was well below average. What sat in our garage now was a 1948 Buick four-door sedan. It offered a straight eight for a power plant, a visor over the two-piece windshield, and standard shift. The nearest it came to being a modern car were its plaid vinyl seat covers. A sickly green, it looked like a beetle with fenders and sounded like a wounded buffalo.

Around the time I began eighth grade and whenever he was in a good mood, which was usually the case after mass and a late Sunday morning breakfast, my dad would often take me down to the parking lots next to Municipal Stadium. There I would learn the fine and somewhat tricky art of driving a standard shift, while Dad gritted his teeth as I let out the clutch in first, and the entire car shuddered. I graduated to road driving on those Sunday afternoons when my mother and brother left earlier with one of my aunts for the ride out to my uncle's cottage in Bethlehem. The wisdom of his actions notwithstanding, and though he had confidence in me, he was not about to jeopardize their welfare, even on virtually deserted country roads. The only disturbing event I experienced on those rural journeys occurred when a blue jay went off course and flew into the door mirror on my side. Though I grew up to be a fairly fast (but cautious) driver, I was so preoccupied trying to maneuver the green beetle that I had no desire for speed.

Confidence grew as the lessons progressed, and that helped set the stage for what was clearly a risky and irresponsible decision. One Saturday evening a month my father, his brother Jim, their cousins Phil and Hugo, and their wives played pinochle. The card party rotated from house to house. On one of those evenings early in June of 1956, just a couple of weeks shy of my graduation, my Uncle Jim and Aunt Rose picked up my parents for a night of bidding, melding, and trumping. They dropped off my cousin Jim to keep me company. My brother had already left for the canteen dance, so we were on our own.

My cousin Jim, an only child, and I, born only nineteen days apart, were pretty much like brothers in many respects, except that he was more creative, smarter, and taller. So much for equal genetic distribution. We sat on the wall of my driveway and waved good-bye to our parents with innocent smiles on our faces, but evil in our hearts. Everyone was gone, and the old Buick was in the garage. On that June night, Jim and I hit the road, and, as it turned out, nearly everything else in our path.

I nervously lifted the garage door beneath the master bedroom. Before I got behind the wheel, my more creative cousin thought we should mark the precise spot where the car stood so as not to raise suspicion when my parents returned. From the cupboards at the rear of the garage, where there were enough canned and dry goods to maintain a small battalion for a couple of months, Jim grabbed some cans of Jolly Green Giant beans and positioned them where each tire rested. With cans in place, door open, and a pillow from our couch under my rear end, it was time to go.

I started her up, gently let out the clutch, and slowly moved the forty or so feet to the street. Our under-aged, unlicensed, unthinking adventure had begun. So far, so good I thought as we turned right, headed toward the end of the street, and then took a right onto short but steep Moreland Avenue. And then, no more than thirty seconds into our little excursion, the recklessness of what I was doing threw my nervous system into high gear. The car seemed so much bigger. The enormous hood of this untamed beast seemed to move as if it had a will of its own. As the dead end of Moreland Avenue loomed, I realized I had to take a quick left onto Mount Vernon Avenue or the car would stall. Getting the car to move on a level surface was one thing, but having to stop on a severe upgrade, then let that clutch out while giving it enough gas to prevent it from rolling backwards, was something I hadn't yet learned and hadn't anticipated. I made it around the corner, but my hands were sweating. Jim, having read my thoughts, kept trying to slide under the dashboard. I thought I heard the clicking of rosary beads.

What my head didn't realize, but my heart did, was that this was neither a spin around an empty parking lot, nor was it a ride along a country lane where all I had to do was follow the gentle curves and watch out for a rabbit, a piece of farm machinery, or a herd of cows crossing the road on their way to the milking parlor. A residential neighborhood offered countless distractions: narrow streets, sharp turns, and kids playing in their front yards.

I took a sharp right up Lee Street, still in second gear, and, a few seconds later, yet another right at the top of the hill onto relatively level Gaylord Drive where I immediately pulled over. Our giddy laughter didn't fool either of us. Jim and I were emotionally drained. We knew we had to get back to my house before something bad happened. If I continued along Gaylord Drive for a couple of hundred yards, I would have no choice but to go down Wayland Avenue which would bring us out next to my house. That meant I would have to negotiate my favorite sledding hill, but the Buick wasn't my Flexible Flyer. I slowly turned around in someone's driveway and carefully retraced my path.

In the two minutes it took to get home, I realized I had trapped myself into having to perform yet one more driving maneuver for which I was unprepared. I would have to drive a few feet past our driveway in order to back into our garage. This placed the car on a downgrade which meant I would have to shift into reverse, take my foot off the brake, place it on the accelerator, let the clutch out, and give the car enough gas to overcome the pull of the hill, all in a split second. If I failed, the car could end up in the middle of the street, making it a great target for any vehicle roaring up and around the sharp curve in front of my house—or, worse yet, I could lose control and let the car roll through the woods and down into the pond where we would join the frogs and dragon flies.

I held my breath, jumped on the gas, let out the clutch, and the car leapt backward, nudging the stonewall alongside our garage. At least I was safely in the driveway. Jim got out to guide me. I rolled forward a few feet, cocked the wheel, and ever so slowly backed into the tight confines of the garage, slightly scraping a fender as Jim called out directions to get me between the cans of beans. I finally got the car in position, shifted to neutral, and set the emergency brake. My shaking hand could barely find the key as I reached to turn off the ignition.

We inspected the damage. It was minor, and, considering the beating the car took in the parking lot at Chase Brass and Copper, I was pretty sure it would go unnoticed. The giddy laughter resumed, but not for long. The damage might have gone unnoticed but the deed would not. For some reason my brother had returned early from the dance. Seeing the garage door open and the car gone, he immediately called my parents. He was on the phone as I climbed the cellar stairs. Fortunately, he was speaking with my mother. Both had instantly and correctly assessed the situation.

With a broad smile on his face, he handed me the receiver. So much for fraternal loyalty. My mother had to keep her voice down as she hissed through her tightly clenched jaw. After asking if everything was all right, she said, "I won't tell your father, but God help you if you ever pull a stunt like that again."

Jim wisely headed for home. I "thanked" my brother for calling and nervously watched television for a while but saw nothing. I made sure I went to bed before they got home, but sleep didn't come easily. Certain that she would tell my father, I lay there wondering what it was going to be like to spend the rest of my life in a wheelchair.

We all went to mass the next morning, where I prayed hard— really hard. But before we left for church, I had noticed, except for one steely glare from my mother when I walked into the kitchen, there was none of what I had anticipated. My father gave absolutely no signal that he was aware of my doings the previous evening. After church, we had our usual hearty Sunday breakfast. Still nothing. Certainly I had to have been the topic of the previous night's pillow talk. My father was a little better than my mother at keeping his emotions masked, but still he was an easy read. Mom, my co-conspirator, had apparently kept her promise.

For the next forty-eight years of my life, there was never a mention of our ride in the green beetle. But from that day on, there was a little stronger bond between my mother and me. She had begun to mellow and I never again violated her trust.

Mr. Delaney Redux

Along with my senior classes, every year or so I taught a class of sophomores composed largely of non-academic kids. I was always in search of writing assignments that would provide greater incentive than usual. In the early eighties I proposed that they write a thank-you letter to someone whose actions or influence, if only for a moment, made a significant impact on their lives. This would be a real letter. I would supply the envelopes and stamps and mail them. I asked that they try and keep immediate family off their list. Any letter thanking a boyfriend, girlfriend, or best friend for "being there" was absolutely prohibited. I offered the suggestion that they needn't have to look for a big moment; that sometimes a small gesture can brighten our lives and give us greater faith in our fellow human beings. Implicit in the assignment was also the thought that we so often fail to thank people for the good that they do. Virtue may be its own reward, but it doesn't hurt to recognize it. In order to boost their enthusiasm and effort, I promised that I would also write such a letter, and, after reviewing it with them, would mail it with all the rest.

What inspired the assignment was a long-overdue letter to my sixth grade teacher, Jack Delaney, not only for his inspired teaching and the joy of his company, but also for two small gestures that touched me deeply.

On a June afternoon in seventh grade, Mr. Nolan walked to the blackboard on our left, picked up a piece of chalk, and instead of going into a windup, listed those seventh graders who would serve in the Honor Guard for the eighth grade graduating class. Aside from the stars in the program next to the names of the graduates (two for first honors, one for second), the Honor Guard was the only academic recognition offered by our school. We never had an honor roll, let alone silly public relations gimmicks like bumper stickers to proclaim our accomplishments. Our letter grades, and that all-important left side of the report card, said all that was necessary for us and our parents to know where we stood, though we all knew early on that Kathy Galvin and Sharon Collette were destined to be our valedictorian and salutatorian. The list completed, Nolan put the chalk back on the ledge and returned to the front of the class, but my eyes remained on the board.

My name was not on the list. I was not surprised. Much of my effort that year had been like my early experiences at the plate in Little League. There I stood, with the go-ahead run on third and a full count, praying that the overgrown knuckle-dragger on the mound fifty feet away would walk me. Unfortunately, I spent too much of seventh grade watching that third pitch go right over the middle of the plate. Though my overall record was less than stellar, it was still respectable. Nevertheless, I believed I had gotten what I deserved. Though the mystery of how those honored were chosen did cross my mind, we were never actually told how they were selected. Was it a fair and impartial process? Were there mistakes and oversights? I was soon to learn someone else had the same questions.

What was even more difficult to understand and explain was my reaction to that moment. As Mr. Nolan resumed class, I felt the salty sting of tears. I was angry that I had apparently screwed up, but there was no great sense of loss. There was no sobbing, no gasping for air, yet I silently sat there as the tears continued to flow. This was particularly baffling because I was not a crier, and what was even more disconcerting was that the other half of my consciousness was trying to figure out what was going on. I immediately covered my face and pretended to yawn and rub my "tired" eyes. Mr. Nolan didn't seem to notice my emotional outpouring, and none of my classmates reacted either at that moment or later after school.

I had never given the Honor Guard any priority, in fact I didn't give a hoot. I think the tears came not because of my failure to be chosen, but more as a form of self- retribution for my cavalier attitude about school that year. With the exception of Mr. Delaney's class the previous year, I rarely pushed myself, though I did uphold my own standard, which was usually above average. I never consciously sought recognition, but when the possibility was taken away, I clearly saw something in myself which I not only disliked, but also something for which I was solely responsible. It wasn't about getting an award; it was about not giving myself a chance to earn it.

When I arrived at school the next morning, the graduating eighth graders were milling around in preparation for the class picture. I went to homeroom and prepared to clean out my desk. At noon we would be out the door for another carefree summer.

Moments after Miss Fitzgerald took attendance, Mr. Delaney appeared in the doorway and asked if he could see me. His broad grin allayed some of my usual paranoia, but our bland conversation—How are your mom and dad? Going to play Little League this summer?—on the way to the office didn't shed any light on what was happening. He asked me to wait in the hallway and then reappeared with Mr. Carrington, our principal, who said only "Good morning" and simply smiled. Mr. Delaney asked me if I would be able to get home, change into a tie and jacket, and get back to the school in a half hour. I silently nodded. "By the way," he said, "You're going to be in the Honor Guard." I was stunned, but in the rush of the moment, I didn't have time to think about much other than to race home.

I blew in the front door and blurted out the news on the way to my closet. My mother seemed pleased but not surprised. I was dressed in minutes, but neither of us knew how to tie a tie. I usually wore a clip-on to church, but this occasion called for one of my father's better ties. As we struggled to tie a knot in the living room, Al the mailman came up the front steps. We immediately recruited him. He stood behind me and tied a perfect Windsor knot, which uses the maximum amount of tie, and prevented it from hanging down to my knees. My mother actually gave me a kiss on the cheek as I flew out the door.

We ushered parents and stood at attention at the end of each row when the National Anthem was played. An hour later the ceremonies were over, and I headed back upstairs for the last moments of the seventh grade class and promotion to eighth grade. I found I wasn't going anywhere. I would be in Miss Fitzgerald's room again for my final year.

On the way out of school a few classmates inquired about the rush and the dress clothing. I just told them that an extra usher was needed. My family believed in quiet pride. Boasting was not approved. I walked home with a smile, both for the unexplained honor and in anticipation of yet another summer of baseball and playing in the woods. But the best part of that smile belonged to Mr. Delaney. I was later told that, feeling there had been a mistake, he had questioned the absence of my name on the list. To this day I am not fully convinced that I deserved the honor. But on that June morning I had no doubt that Jack Delaney was just about the finest person I had ever known.

His thoughtfulness wouldn't end there.

Tryouts for the eighth grade baseball team were held the following spring. We also had a sixth grade team. Mr. Delaney coached both. The competition for the eighth grade team was stiff because talented seventh graders were also eligible to play. What would make my competition even more formidable was my own sudden loss of concentration.

When tryouts began, I was reasonably confident that I could make the team. I had played on the sixth grade team, was a starter in Little League the previous summer, and had played countless pick-up games at the park since fifth grade. When there weren't enough for a regular game, we would play a game we called Flies Out. One boy would toss the ball out of his hand and hit it to the one or two others in the outfield. The rules were simple. When a participant caught three fly balls and three grounders without bobbling the ball, that player would become the hitter. All of our practice gave us the skills to play well. Delaney's job would not be easy.

I was a fair hitter, had a good arm, above average speed, and could catch most of whatever was hit at me. But for reasons that defied logic, I started having trouble catching fly balls. Mr. Delaney had placed me in center field because I could cover a lot of ground. When he took out the fungo bat and started belting long, high shots, I suddenly found myself misjudging the ball. I was either over-running or underplaying it. The harder I tried, the worse it got, and the craziness and frustration didn't help. I think the answer lay somewhere in the idea that we sometimes get in the way of our reflexes, which, especially when well trained, will usually do what they are supposed to do. I made the mistake of thinking about what I was doing.

My experience was not unique. Even major leaguers occasionally run into similar situations. A few years ago Yankee second baseman Chuck Knoblauch began to struggle with making the throw to first, so much so that he was moved to the outfield. Thankfully my problem eventually passed, but that would happen too late. Mr. Delaney had to cut me. I knew he had no choice. That realization didn't make things any easier when, a couple of weeks later, some of my best friends wore their uniforms to class for the first game of the season. My hazel eyes became a little greener as the time neared for their early dismissal.

At two-thirty the players picked up their gloves and shuffled out the door to the bus waiting at the front of the school. As the last one passed through, I dropped my head. Then I heard his voice in the doorway. "Excuse me, Miss Fitzgerald. I think I forgot to tell you that Jerry Joyell is the team manager." Pretending that she was surprised by what I'm sure was already set up in the teachers' lunchroom, Miss Fitzgerald said in a stagy voice. "Oh, certainly. Jerry, you may leave." Script completed, I was out the door. Mr. Delaney gave me a team cap and told me to take care of all the gear, hit some ground balls to the infielders, and sit next to him on the bench. Nothing could wipe the grin off my face for the rest of that day.

It has been my experience that such people are rare. His thoughtfulness didn't end with me, but it influenced me enough that I tried to emulate it with those I taught and coached. Sometimes they appreciated it; sometimes they didn't. But what really mattered was that I knew Mr. Delaney would be pleased with me, and that alone was reward enough.

As I got older and bumped into him downtown, at his request, Mr. Delaney became Jack. And when I saw him at high school basketball games (he coached two Waterbury high schools), my reaction was the same that we all have for those who were once a special part of our daily lives. The handshake and hug were all that was needed.

Years later I read my letter to Mr. Delaney to my students who gave their approval. I took all the letters to the post office after school, and, with the nervous expectation of a kid who was anticipating a reply to his Christmas letter to Santa, I waited.

Some of my students got replies, but I never did. Curious, though reluctant to hear bad news, I checked with people in

Waterbury to see how Jack was doing. My fears were confirmed when I learned Mr. Delaney had suffered a serious stroke in 1977. I was crushed. It was more than painfully difficult for me to accept that this man, who was only in his early fifties, and the essence of vitality, energy, and joviality, whose kindness and inspiration had touched so many, was struck low by such a fate. My letter had arrived too late.

Because I read *The Hartford Courant*, I had always relied on my father to keep me apprised of goings on in Waterbury. He faithfully checked the obituaries in the *Waterbury Republican* for news he felt I should know. But my mother suddenly died on November 26, 1990. The loss of his partner of over fifty years, and the adjustment to a new way of life, changed his daily routine for a while. And that was why, some five weeks later, he missed the news of Jack Delaney's passing on January 2, 1991.

Only at this writing did I learn all the facts from his daughter Mary Ellen. During our phone conversations, the old feelings came rushing back. She informed me that he had received my letter but was unable to reply. How I wished it could have been otherwise, but then I realized that it didn't have to be. All I had to do was whisper his name in my heart, and he would be there.

Chapter 31

Ave et vale Bunker Hill School

Mrs. Delaney's rump lightly bounced along the piano bench as she pounded out the melody to "I Hear America Singing." She was a citywide music teacher, not related to Jack, but had almost as much energy. The lyrics by poet Walt Whitman and music by Harvey Gaul were more than a little challenging for her to teach and us to learn. We tried for three-part harmony, but I'm not sure a bunch of giddy eighth graders ever reached that lofty goal.

The weeks of rehearsal passed quickly and before I knew it I was donning my charcoal gray suit and slipping into my white bucks. My father had wisely tied a neat Windsor knot the night before. Most working fathers would not be able to attend our graduation at ten that morning.

My mother and I walked to the school together, then parted as she went to the gymnasium at the rear, and I remained in front for the class pictures. A few minutes later we filed into the tiny gym to the tune of the "Connecticut March." We bowed our heads and Reverend Murphy gave the invocation, then we all rose to sing "The Star Spangled Banner." After salutatorian Sharon Collette greeted the parents, we filed up to our elevated position just beneath the stage. Mrs. Delaney hit the keys, and much to her delight, we hit the notes.

The centerpiece of the ceremony successfully completed, we filed back to our seats. Valedictorian Kathy Galvin bid all a farewell, then the president of the Board of Aldermen began to distribute our diplomas. As my name was called, I reminded myself to take with the left and shake with the right. We again took our position near the stage, sang our fealty song, then filed out of the gym and awaited our parents for the mandatory photo sessions.

Later that evening, Sandy Pinsky threw a helluva graduation party—lots of hot dogs, hamburgers, hugs, kisses, and dancing. But not to the usual selection we heard at the canteens. That night we tripped the light fantastic to the tunes of the Platters, Fats Domino, Buddy Holly, and Elvis. We rocked and rolled all night long, but not to our parents' tunes. This was *our* music.

The times, indeed, were a-changin'.

Chapter 32

What though that radiance which was once so bright
Be now forever taken from my sight,
Though nothing can bring back the hour
Of splendour in the grass, of glory in the flower;
We will grieve not, rather find
Strength in what remains behind . . .

William Wordsworth

The reunion was an unqualified success. As the Four Lads sang "Moments To Remember," we all agreed that the events of that day had far exceeded our expectations. For a moment, we really were able to resurrect the memories and feelings that had made childhood such a special time in our lives.

But amid the music and dancing, I couldn't shake one question that had been discussed earlier that evening: Why would members of the older generation be so reluctant to trade places with the younger? Earlier, classmate Kathy Galvin said she thought it was because we were so secure then, and today's kids simply are not. No argument there. The disintegrating family unit, parental hovering and/or neglect, overwhelming pressures arising from exploitation by the media and business interests—all help rule out for youngsters the kind of childhood they are entitled to.

I felt compelled to ask myself: Is it possible in today's society to give kids the kind of childhood we enjoyed? Without giving them the same values, attitudes, and learning, as well as the same restraints and responsibilities that our parents gave us, I doubt it. Those fundamentals are the stuff of childhood, the same things we need to become well-adjusted adults. Why did we let so much of it slip away? No one answer is correct, but I know that if we don't start to honestly examine the problem and reverse some of the disturbing societal trends that have developed over the last few decades, childhood, as it should be, will be little more than a memory.

My wife pulled me out of my dark reflections and back onto the dance floor. Appropriately enough, just as our canteens ended years ago, the plaintive strains of "Goodnight Sweetheart, Goodnight" told us the evening was over. When the music stopped and the teary-eyed good-byes began, we knew that we had to do it again in 2006. The deejay was packing his gear as my wife and I slipped out the door into the chill September night. Over by the pond a lonely katydid was still calling for a mate to keep him company.

The evening's euphoria still with me as we climbed into the car, I gave myself a moment while I waited for the fogged windshield to clear. The radio was on, but I wasn't listening. I was trying to put a cap on the whole experience when some words of Sophocles came to mind: "Often it is not until the night that we can know how splendid was the day."

Made in the USA
Charleston, SC
11 February 2015